BIRTH OF THE FEW

BIRTH OF THE FEW

16 October 1939 - RAF Spitfires
win their first battle with
the Luftwaffe

HENRY BUCKTON

—— *from the notes of* ——

Group Captain
Sir Hugh Dundas
CBE DSO DFC DL

Airlife
England

First published in the UK in 1998
by Airlife Publishing Ltd

British Library Cataloguing-in-Publication Data
A catalogue record for this book
is available from the British Library

ISBN 1 85310 972 X

Typeset by Phoenix Typesetting, Ilkley, West Yorkshire.

Printed in Great Britain by St Edmundsbury Press Ltd, Bury St Edmunds, Suffolk

Airlife Publishing Ltd
101 Longden Road, Shrewsbury, SY3 9EB, England.

FOREWORD

Memories – they have served us well over the past few months, as the people of Western Europe, and beyond, have looked back over half a century, first to the fiftieth anniversary of the Normandy invasion, then to victory in Europe. We have learned from these occasions, that looking back at and remembering great events, which have shaped our lives and destinies, is a process which goes far beyond mere sentiment and nostalgia. Indeed, it is a process which is essential if we are to understand and preserve the values which underpin our heritage.

This book records the memories of many men and women whom, either as participants or as eye-witnesses, were involved in an attack by German bombers against ships of the Royal Navy in the Firth of Forth during the afternoon of 16 October 1939. It was the first time in the Second World War that German bombers raiding the United Kingdom were shot down by Royal Air Force fighters.

The story of that raid, as it unfolds in this book, will perhaps surprise those who read it as much by its revelation of what went wrong as what went right. There is nothing surprising about that, I suppose, for the whole elaborate air defence system was being tested in earnest almost for the first time. What is surprising is that the two German bombers which fell that day were shot down by Spitfires of the Auxiliary Air Force, the 'Week-end Flyers,' whose squadrons had so crucially supplemented the thin blue line of regular Hurricane and Spitfire squadrons which made up Fighter Command at the outbreak of the war. And so the crack Luftwaffe crews sent by Göring to register a victory in British air space were taken on by young men who, only a month before, had been primarily engaged in civilian occupations – farmers, lawyers, businessmen, artisans. Furthermore, while the professionally manned radar early warning system failed to contribute much to the interceptions, the Observer Corps, manned by civilian volunteers, provided the control centres with prompt and accurate plots of the bombers' progress.

5

And so the memories evoked by this particular episode may usefully serve to remind us all of the critically important part played by the voluntary services in winning the Second World War and thus in preserving our freedom and democratic way of life. We should rejoice and take pride in the fact that the tradition of voluntary service lives on strongly today. Indeed it is exemplified by the author of this book and by tens of thousands of patriotic men and women like him.

Group Captain Sir Hugh Dundas
CBE DSO DFC DL
May 1995

ACKNOWLEDGEMENTS

The first acknowledgement of course goes to Group Captain Sir Hugh Dundas, without whom this book would never have been written. The idea for the book and much of the information and research within its covers, was orchestrated before Henry Buckton was even born.

Thanks to all those who helped Sir Hugh with his research, especially Douglas Farquhar, Jim Morton, George Denholm and Sigmund Storp, all of whom took part in the action over Edinburgh that day. Also, George Ward, who was the Secretary of State for Air in 1957 and Mr J Nerney, Air Historical Branch.

I would also like to thank Howard Watson (Permissions Controller) at Random House (UK) Limited for permission to use the extract from *Flying Start* by Sir Hugh Dundas and publishers Stanley Paul. Thanks also go to Air Vice-Marshal A.V.R. (Sandy) Johnstone CB DFC AE DL RAF (Retd) for allowing me to use information contained in his book, *Spitfire into War* published by William Kimber. Thanks to Bill Campbell, Director of Mainstream Publishing Co. (Edinburgh) Ltd, for allowing the use of information obtained from *This Present Emergency* by Andrew Jeffrey. Thanks to Observer Lieutenant P.J. Proost from Royal Observer Corps Headquarters; and Vic Campden MBE from No 24 Group (Edinburgh) Royal Observer Corps Association. Thanks also go to Peter Vasey, Head of the Historical Search Section, at the Scottish Record Office, The National Archives of Scotland: and to the Keeper of the Records of Scotland for the use of documents and material stored in Scottish Office file HH50/5. A number of quotes are also taken from 'Hutchinson's Pictorial History of the War' for which thanks go to Michael Virtue of Virtue and Company Limited, Publishers, Hole House, Haltwhistle, Northumberland.

I would also like to thank the following people who have helped in some way: George Conway MBE AEA, Hugh Barkla, Ian Brown, Jack Berry, David T. Watson, James Thomson Dick, Jas. C. P. Cessford, John Kerr, Angus McKenzie, Francis Rennie, John Donaldson, Chris M.

ACKNOWLEDGEMENTS

Prentice, Mrs M. Conyon, Mrs Jessica Boak, Rita Darling, Mrs A. Anderson, James Marshall, James Cranston, James Sime, Thos W. Stewart, James Clark, Mr J. Hall-Livingstone, Mowbray G. Pearson, T. S. Johnston, Ms J. Montgomery, Mrs Sheila Laird, Jas. H. F. Ross, Peter Smith, Mrs. Barbara Sibbald, George Mullay, H. G. Niven (Hon. Secretary of the 602 Squadron Museum, Glasgow).

A very special thanks to author Andrew Jeffrey, who made available his own research into the Forth Raid, for this book. Through him, thanks go to Helmut Pohle for his letters and memories.

Thanks also to the 'Few' pilots, who took part in the action that day and have helped with the book in some way: Dunlop Urie, Marcus Robinson, Paul Webb and Alastair Grant (all 602 Squadron).

Another big thank you goes to Brian Farish, who has supplied photographs, drawn plans and even written a section of the text.

Finally, thanks go to author Richard Bickers for writing the short dedication to Sir Hugh Dundas.

CONTENTS

INTRODUCTION

In putting pen to paper and beginning to write this book, I hardly know where to begin. The fact that it was written at all, now seems quite incredible, especially when one considers that it is based largely on a half-finished manuscript, which lay forlorn and forgotten for over thirty years. Ultimately, it tells the story of a single day in 1939, which catapulted the 'Weekend Flyers' of the Auxiliary Air Force, into the stuff of legends. It is also the story of a search for information, the truth about events, and a quest that tirelessly spans decades to arrive at its final conclusion. It is also, I believe, an object lesson in the power of destiny.

The day in question was 16 October 1939. In Britain, it was the last day when petrol would cost 1/6d a gallon – on the following day it was raised to 1/8d. Restaurant car services on the railways, suspended at the beginning of the war, were restored on L.M.S. trains and the company announced that the standard price of meals taken on trains would be 2/6d. Eros was moved from Piccadilly Circus to a safe place for the duration of the war. On the Western Front the Germans attacked along a 4-mile front east of the Moselle, occupying high ground on which the French Army had maintained a line of observation posts. In Washington, Senator Worth-Clark of Idaho made a speech in the Senate bitterly attacking Great Britain for her 'historic misdeeds'.

On 16 October 1939 at the Luftwaffe airfield of Westerland, on the island of Sylt, twelve Ju 88 bombers prepared for a raid against Great Britain. The war was now into its second month and this was to be the first Nazi air raid over mainland Britain.

The leader of the formation was *Hauptmann* Helmut Pohle. He was born in 1907, so he was aged between thirty-two and thirty-three – an interesting age in the Nazi Luftwaffe hierarchy at that time. He had served in Berlin, as General Staff Officer at the Air Ministry, and had fought during the Spanish Civil War.

After his years' of training and indoctrination as an officer of Germany's new professional Air Force, Pohle was about to be tested in the fire. He had every reason to feel confident. He also, had every reason to feel honoured.

One of the other planes in the formation was commanded by *Oberleutnant* Sigmund Storp. He was born in 1914. He was also a regular professional officer of the new German Air Force. He served throughout the Spanish Civil War and was awarded the Officers' Cross for his conduct during those operations.

Meanwhile, in the Turnhouse Sector of 13 Group, Fighter Command, two fighter squadrons waited, as they waited every day at various states of readiness. They were Scotland's two original Auxiliary Air Force squadrons. At Turnhouse was 603 (City of Edinburgh) Squadron. At Drem was 602 (City of Glasgow) Squadron.

At Turnhouse was Flight Lieutenant Patsy Gifford. Two weeks' earlier he had been a practising solicitor, living at Castle Douglas. But if he had a slow-speed job, he had high-speed inclinations. He owned a Frazer-Nash which, he claimed, would do 'ninety in third'. He was a good shot and a good games player. He had two sisters who were much admired by his fellow officers, and a squad of pretty girl friends.

At Drem was Flight Lieutenant George Cannon Pinkerton, a thirty-year-old fruit farmer (until two weeks ago) from Houston, Renfrewshire. His wife, to whom he had only recently been married, and his brother were running his farm for him.

Pohle and his Ju 88s were heading north-west along a bomber trail which was to become well-worn in the following years. At a certain point, when Pohle the General Staff Officer must have believed his formation to be certainly undetected, two squadrons of fighter planes were scrambled to intercept. Solicitor Gifford and fruit-farmer Pinkerton were in the lead.

The enemy bombers emerged near the Forth Bridge, flying low over Edinburgh's roof tops. A mirror in the residence of the Lord Provost received a direct hit from a machine-gun bullet. Coincidentally, a couple of years later the Lord Provost was Will Darling – corset maker to three queens – and Honorary Air Commodore to 603 Squadron.

By tea-time Pohle and Storp were prisoners-of-war: Gifford and Pinkerton were Britain's first two victorious fighter pilots over Britain. The solicitor and the farmer had downed the two chosen Luftwaffe regulars.

From Dowding came the signal: 'Well done. First blood to the Auxiliaries!'

16 October 1939 was an important day of debuts. The first Nazi air raid over mainland Britain; the first time Spitfires were engaged against the enemy in battle; the first German aircraft shot down over Britain

11

during the Second World War; the first Luftwaffe raiders taken prisoner; the first successful British pilots above their homeland; 'First Blood to the Auxiliaries'.

Here then is the main theme to the narrative; focussing on the first Nazi raid over mainland Britain, and the men of the Auxiliary Air Force who were destined to shoot down the first German aircraft over home territory.

Indeed, you may ask, this might be a historical episode of some considerable interest to the aviation fraternity, but why should it concern the average reader, some fifty years later? The answer to this and other questions are manyfold. The most obvious being its place in what was Britain's darkest hour. We've all heard of 'The Few', the pilots who protected these islands against the huge Luftwaffe formations, principally during the Battle of Britain. Undoubtedly, 16 October 1939 was the date on which the romance began: 'the birth of The Few'. What was more important, was the fact that the successful pilots on this day were auxiliaries; men who but a few short weeks before had been engaged in their civilian jobs and had enjoyed flying at weekends as members of the twenty Auxiliary Air Force squadrons.

So where does Henry Buckton fit into the story, you may ask. In many ways I have been a spiritual descendant to those heroes of old, along with many others having kept that spirit very much in the present as members of today's Royal Auxiliary Air Force. In the 1930s the solicitor and the fruit-farmer toiled and laboured during the week, keeping up appearances as it were; after all, a fellow had to eat. At the weekend they donned their flying suits and entered into the world of what must have been 'Britain's most exclusive club'. In the 1990s, members of the Royal Auxiliary Air Force continue in a similar vein. Take the squadron to which I belonged as an example, No 4626 (County of Wiltshire) Aeromedical Evacuation Squadron. This is a happy band of airmen and airwomen who are the 'Weekend Flyers' of today. Doctors, nurses, hoteliers, insurance agents, a London Underground train driver, a ballroom dancer and even a graphic designer: notably me! We may in spirit be weekend flyers, although not in practice. The last flying squadrons of the RAuxAF were disbanded in 1957. There are no longer any auxiliary units where personnel actually take the controls. Our flying was done mainly aboard a Hercules from our base at RAF Lyneham in Wiltshire, practising our role as aeromeds.

When it was first formed at Princess Alexandra Hospital, RAF Wroughton, on 9 September 1983, the squadron's basic task was to provide trained medical escorts, men and women, for the evacuation of battle casualties during war or other national emergency, and to reinforce the existing RAF Aeromedical Evacuation organisations, in particular their regular compatriots of No 1 Air Evacuation Squadron. The squadron could be called upon to deploy independently to areas within the UK or overseas. Over the years, personnel from the squadron have flown some three million miles, undertaking peacetime aeromedical evacuations from almost all parts of the world in which one finds British servicemen: Denmark, Germany, Norway, Cyprus, Turkey, East Africa, Hong Kong, Ascension Island, the Falklands, Belize, the United States, Canada, Northern Ireland and the Shetland Isles.

On January 1991, No 4626 Squadron continued the legend, when they became the first auxiliary unit since the end of the Second World War to be mobilised and sent on active service. This happened during the Gulf War when the entire unit suddenly found themselves in Saudi Arabia. One morning they were getting up for work, as they usually did. A few days later, they were getting up for war. But that of course, is a completely different story.

I trust this is all proof of my pedigree and eligibility as the writer of this historic account. I am also a keen historian and have for some time collected information on all aspects of auxiliary affairs in the hope that one day I can complete a blow-by-blow account of the organisation from its inception to the present. Many squadron histories already exist, along with an account of the twenty flying squadrons. There was of course, and still is, much more to the Royal Auxiliary Air Force than the original flying squadrons and that is why there is a necessity to write the whole story. This book however, is not it, although my notes and contacts were very useful in its composition.

Another of my passions, as I hope this book bears testimony, is the power of the written word. This passion is another link in the chain of circumstances surrounding the creation of this work, as indeed was the publication of my first major book, *Forewarned is Forearmed* in 1993. *Forewarned is Forearmed* was an official tribute and history of the Royal Observer Corps (ROC), in which I had served for many years during the 1980s. During the Battle of Britain the Observer Corps was very much the eyes and ears of Fighter Command. The cocktail of radar and the Observer Corps was a lethal brew for the Luftwaffe, as it meant their movements were at all times detected. Our fighter squadrons were able to intercept the invader, as and where they appeared in our skies. In September 1991 the ROC was 'Stood Down' after sixty-six years of service and I took it upon myself to write its history in order to raise money for the Benevolent Fund. In writing the book I thought it would be a good idea to contact some of the fighter pilots who had benefited from ROC tracks during the Second World War. I immediately thought of two of my greatest heroes – Air Vice-Marshal Johnnie Johnson and Group Captain Sir Hugh Dundas – and wondered whether they would oblige. Initially I approached the Battle of Britain Fighter Association, asking its chairman Wing Commander N. Hancock, to put me into contact with these men, along with Air Chief Marshal Sir Christopher Foxley-Norris and Group Captain Tom Gleave. To cut a long story short, I was able to contact all of these Second World War pilots, and all four of them contributed to my book, reflecting their admiration and respect for the now defunct Corps. Without digressing too much, this was yet another link in our story.

In late 1993, after the publication of *Forewarned is Forearmed*, I began to think more and more about the possibility of researching a complete history of the Royal Auxiliary Air Force. But where does one begin? Immediately I thought of Sir Hugh Dundas. He had very kindly supported me with the ROC book, so I felt confident that he would be interested to learn about a project on the RAuxAF, with which he had a far greater connection.

Hugh Spencer Lisle Dundas, known as 'Cocky', was without question one of the greatest names in auxiliary history. He was born at Barnborough Hall near Doncaster on 22 July 1920. His family was not particularly wealthy, although he grew up within a circle of relatives and friends who still held vast fortunes and estates and whose lavish Victorian lifestyles were only slightly disturbed by the disruption of the First World War and its resulting social mutiny at home. There were still large houses where old country families were waited on by endless numbers of staff, enjoying garden, shooting, tennis and bathing parties, cricket matches, and picnics. It was into this privileged world that Hugh Dundas emerged and to a large extent, so did the Auxiliary Air Force.

In some ways Hugh Dundas was an unlikely hero. His father had been too old to serve during the First World War and most of his family had followed a political career. His interest in things military stemmed from preparatory school at Aysgarth in North Yorkshire, whose library could boast copies of *The Times History of the Great War* and the earlier volumes about the South African War. From their heroic pages Hugh Dundas learned about the great deeds of great Britons and dreamed of the day when his own name would be listed within their honoured ranks, admired by a captivated nation.

Hugh Dundas grew up in the West Riding with his brother John and sisters Elizabeth, Alice and Charmian. Their father rented their house in the village of Cawthorne from a friend who more or less owned the village and the surrounding countryside. When he left school at Stowe in 1938 his ambition to join the Auxiliary Air Force received little encouragement from his family. However, in May 1939 he secured a place with 616 (South Yorkshire) Squadron, as a Pupil Pilot.

616 (South Yorkshire) Squadron, the last of the Auxiliary Air Force flying units, was formed on 1 November 1938. Sir Hugh says of it:

'I belonged to a squadron which went through the fire of failure and defeat before climbing to the heights of success. 616 (South Yorkshire) Squadron was the last to be formed. I joined it in May 1939, when I was eighteen. We had officers posted from 609, 608 and 604 also from the Lincoln special reserve squadron. Our CO, Lord Lincoln, was learning to fly in the summer of 1939 and was posted when war broke out. A regular officer took us over and we – probably bloody-mindedly – took against him. We had Gauntlet biplanes and very, very little experience. By February 1940, we were operational with Spitfires.

'In the spring a Scottish auxiliary took command. We fought for the last week over Dunkirk, without much success but with few casualties. We went back to the north-east coast and had a few local successes.

'On 19 August we moved to Kenley. On 22 August I was shot down in flames over Dover, without seeing what hit me and without firing my guns. When I left Canterbury hospital six days later to go on sick leave the squadron was in pieces. Most of the auxiliaries had been killed, or were in hospital. One or two were in disgrace. The squadron had been pulled out of the line and the CO posted. We reformed in Lincolnshire, under a first rate regular CO, Billy Burton. We were down to five auxiliary pilots, but that five stuck together and constituted the hard core of the squadron which went down to Tangmere in February, 1941, and had a cracking good summer flying with Douglas Bader. I was the last auxiliary to leave the squadron, in September 1941. Of the other four one had been killed, two were prisoners-of-war and another had been promoted to command a squadron.'

In actual fact, Hugh Dundas had really wanted to join his brother John in 609 Squadron, which he had joined before the war. Between 31 May 1940, when he shot down an He 111 and a Do 17 over Dunkirk, and 15 October, when he got a Bf 110 and had won a DFC, John Dundas had destroyed at least twelve enemy aircraft. On November 28 – by which time he was a Flight Lieutenant – he shot down a Bf 109 flown by Helmut Wick, the leading German ace who had fifty-six victories to his name. However, during the battle, Wick's wing man shot John down and he was killed.

On the subject of his brother Sir Hugh writes:

'John Dundas, my elder brother, was the last auxiliary left in 609

Squadron by November 1940. It was a surprise to his family and his friends that he should have become a top-line fighter pilot with thirteen confirmed victories. He was an intellectual, who always passed examinations with success at the earliest possible age, ending up with first class honours at Oxford before his twenty-first birthday. He was vague, irresponsible, late, broke, ubiquitous and charming. He could not drive a car a hundred miles without running into something or running out of fuel. But he learned to fly a Spitfire with great effect. On 28 November 1940, he was leading his flight when 609 Squadron was ordered out high up over the Channel, south of the Isle of Wight. Michael Robinson was leading the squadron. A gaggle of 109s appeared, slightly overhead. It was the Richthofen *Jagdgeschwader*, led by the ranking German fighter ace, Helmut Wick, who claimed fifty-six victories in air combat and who had been decorated by Hitler with the Knight's Cross of the Iron Cross with Oak Leaves. For some minutes the two squadrons manoeuvred, both clawing for height and sun advantage. An arrow formation of 109s dived to attack. A flight of Spitfires wheeled to intercept the attack. John Dundas called "Whoopee – I've got one". The 109s plunged down. A torn parachute was seen streaming down to the sea. Both Wick and Dundas failed to return from this engagement.'

Sir Hugh's ambition to join 609 Squadron was quashed by his own cousin Harald Peake, who had been the CO of 609 since its formation. When 616 Squadron was formed Peake was appointed as its first CO. Harald Peake was looking for suitable recruits and Hugh Dundas found himself in the new Doncaster squadron. As it turned out, Harald Peake never took command of 616 Squadron, because he shortly found himself appointed to the position of Director of the Auxiliary Air Force at the Air Ministry. Instead, the Earl of Lincoln – later to become the Duke of Newcastle – took command. In actual fact Hugh's posting to 616 turned out for the best. His ambition on leaving Stowe in the summer of 1938, as well as joining the Auxiliary Air Force, was to go to Christ Church Oxford, like his brother before him. The only flaw to this plan was the fact that his father would only let him go to Oxford if he could gain a scholarship. His father favoured the idea of professional qualifications and arranged for his son to be articled to the family solicitors, Messrs Newman and Bond, who as it happened, had a branch in Doncaster. Hugh Dundas could now appreciate the fact that studying law in Doncaster had its distinct advantages; notably the chance to fly.

Had it not been for a doctor called O'Malley, this story might never have been written. When Hugh Dundas attempted to join the auxiliaries he failed the medical, without explanation of why he was rejected. Twice more he applied and failed, again without knowing why. On the

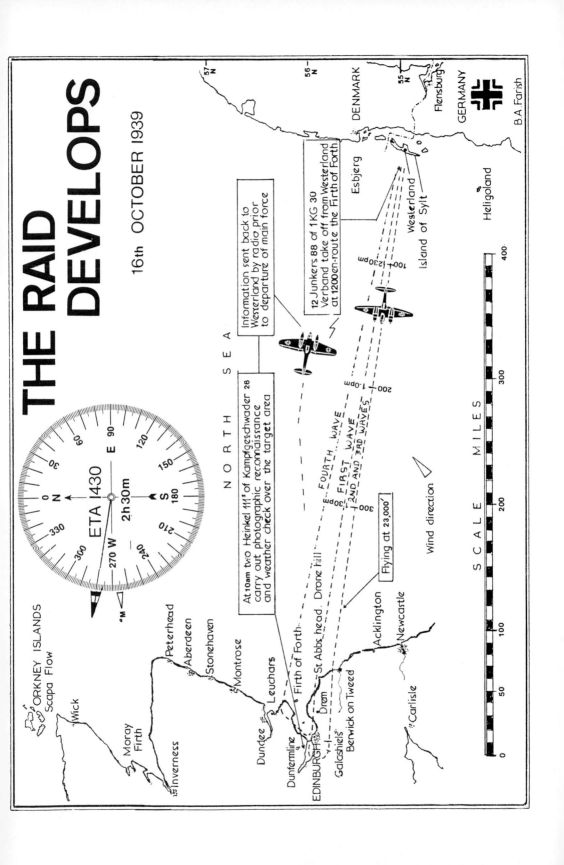

THE RAID DEVELOPS

16th OCTOBER 1939

ETA 1430
2h30m

Information sent back to Westerland by radio prior to departure of main force

12 Junkers 88 of 1KG 30 Verband take off from Westerland at 1200en-route the Firth of Forth

At 10am two Heinkel 111s of Kampfgeschwader 26 carry out photographic reconnaissance and weather check over the target area

Flying at 23,000'

Wind direction

NORTH SEA

ORKNEY ISLANDS
Scapa Flow
Wick
Moray Firth
Inverness
Peterhead
Aberdeen
Stonehaven
Montrose
Dundee
Leuchars
Firth of Forth
Duntermline
EDINBURGH
Galashiels
Dram
St Abbs head. Drone Hill
Berwick on Tweed
Acklington
Newcastle
Carlisle

FOURTH WAVE
FIRST WAVE
2ND AND 3RD WAVES
300
300
200
100
100-1200m
200-1200m

DENMARK
Esbjerg
Westerland
Island of Sylt
Flensburg
GERMANY
Heligoland

57 N
56 N
55 N

B.A.Farish

SCALE MILES
0   50   100   200   300   400

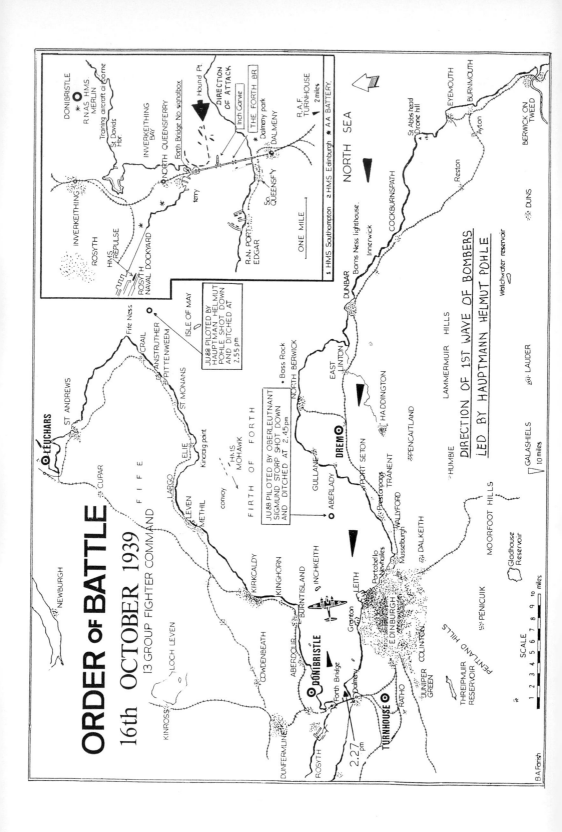

ORDER of BATTLE
16th OCTOBER 1939
13 GROUP FIGHTER COMMAND

NEWBURGH

ST ANDREWS

LEUCHARS

KINROSS

LOCH LEVEN

CUPAR

F I F E

Fife Ness

CRAIL

ANSTRUTHER

PITTENWEEM

ST MONANS

ELIE

Kincraig point

LARGO

LEVEN

METHIL

convoy

FIRTH OF FORTH

ISLE OF MAY

H.M.S. MOHAWK

JU88 PILOTED BY HAUPTMAN HELMUT POHLE SHOT DOWN AND DITCHED AT 2.55 pm

JU88 PILOTED BY OBERLEUTNANT SIGMUND STORP SHOT DOWN AND DITCHED AT 2.45 pm

Bass Rock

North Berwick

GULLANE

ABERLADY

PORT SETON

DREM

EAST LINTON

HADDINGTON

PENCAITLAND

HUMBIE

LAMMERMUIR HILLS

DIRECTION OF 1ST WAVE OF BOMBERS
LED BY HAUPTMANN HELMUT POHLE

GALASHIELS

LAUDER

DUNS

Watchwater reservoir

COCKBURNSPATH

Innerwick

Barns Ness lighthouse

DUNBAR

NORTH SEA

St Abbs head Drone hill

EYEMOUTH

BURNMOUTH

Reston

Ayton

BERWICK ON TWEED

DUNFERMLINE

ROSYTH

Forth Bridge

Dalmeny

2.27 pm

RATHO

TURNHOUSE

COMDENBEATH

ABERDOUR

DONIBRISTLE

Granton

LEITH

Portobello

Newhailes

Musselburgh

DALKEITH

Prestonpans

TRANENT

WALLYFORD

EDINBURGH

JUNIPER GREEN

COLINTON

PENTLAND HILLS

THREIPMUIR RESERVOIR

PENICUIK

Gladhouse Reservoir

MOORFOOT HILLS

KINGHORN

BURNTISLAND

INCHKEITH

KIRKCALDY

SCALE

1 2 3 4 5 6 7 8 9 10 miles

10 miles

B.A. Farish

Inset map (top)

DONIBRISTLE

RNAS HMS MERLIN

Training aircraft airborne

St Davids Hbr.

INVERKEITHING BAY

NORTH QUEENSFERRY

Forth Bridge No. signalbox

Hound Pt.

Inch Garvie

THE FORTH BR.

DIRECTION OF ATTACK

Dalmeny park

DALMENY

R.A.F. TURNHOUSE

AA BATTERY

NORTH SEA

So. QUEENSFY

R.N. PORT EDGAR

ONE MILE

1 HMS Southampton 2 HMS Edinburgh

INVERKEITHING

ROSYTH

HMS REPULSE

ferry

ROSYTH NAVAL DOCKYARD

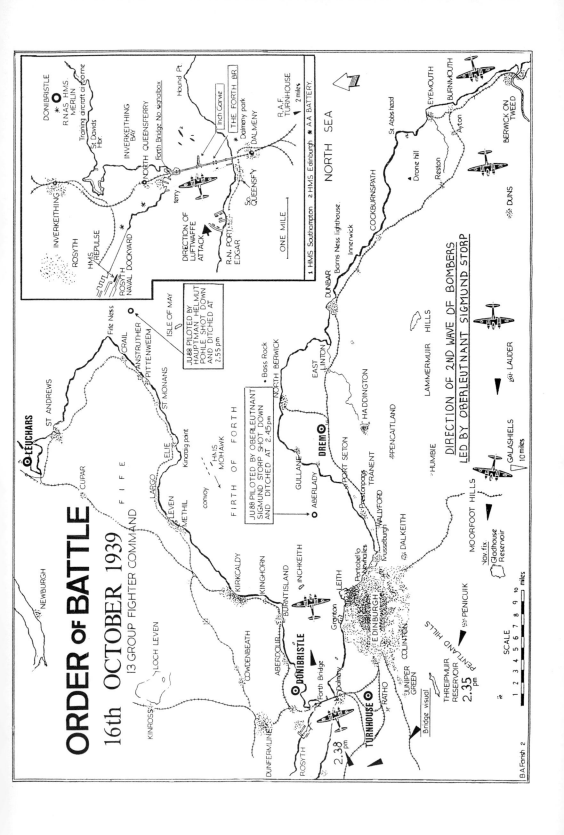

ORDER of BATTLE
16th OCTOBER 1939
13 GROUP FIGHTER COMMAND

NORTH SEA

FIRTH OF FORTH

FIFE

Inset map:
DONIBRISTLE
RNAS HMS. MERLIN
Training aircraft airborne
St Davids Hbr.
INVERKEITHING BAY
NORTH QUEENSFERRY
Forth Bridge No signalbox
Hound Pt
Inch Garvie
THE FORTH BR.
Dalmeny park
Dalmeny
R.A.F. TURNHOUSE
2 miles
AA BATTERY
HMS. REPULSE
INVERKEITHING
ROSYTH
ROSYTH NAVAL DOCKYARD
ferry
So. QUEENSFY
DIRECTION OF LUFTWAFFE ATTACK
R.N. PORT EDGAR
ONE MILE
1 HMS Southampton 2 HMS Edinburgh

Fife Ness
CRAIL
ANSTRUTHER
PITTENWEEM
ST MONANS
ISLE OF MAY
JU88 PILOTED BY HAUPTMAN HELMUT POHLE SHOT DOWN AND DITCHED AT 2.55 pm

ST ANDREWS
CUPAR
LEUCHARS
NEWBURGH
LOCH LEVEN
KINROSS
COWDENBEATH
ABERDOUR
DUNFERMLINE
DONIBRISTLE
Forth Bridge
Dalmeny
ROSYTH

LARGO
LEVEN
ELIE
Kincraig point
METHIL
convoy
H.N.S. MOHAWK
Bass Rock
NORTH BERWICK
GULLANE
ABERLADY
JU88 PILOTED BY OBERLEUTNANT SIGMUND STORP SHOT DOWN AND DITCHED AT 2.45pm

KIRKCALDY
KINGHORN
BURNTISLAND
INCHKEITH
Granton
LEITH
Portobello
Newhaven
Musselburgh
EDINBURGH
COLINTON
JUNIPER GREEN
Bridge visual
2.38 pm
TURNHOUSE
RATHO
2.35 pm

PORT SETON
Prestonpans
TRANENT
WALLYFORD
DALKEITH
EAST LINTON
HADDINGTON
PENCAITLAND
HUMBIE
DREM

THREIPMUIR RESERVOIR
PENTLAND HILLS
PENICUIK
MOORFOOT HILLS
Nav. fix
Gladhouse Reservoir

DUNBAR
Burns Ness lighthouse
Innerwick
COCKBURNSPATH
Drone hill
St Abbs head
Reston
Ayton
EYEMOUTH
BURNMOUTH
BERWICK ON TWEED
DUNS
LAMMERMUIR HILLS
LAUDER
GALASHIELS
10 miles

DIRECTION OF 2ND WAVE OF BOMBERS LED BY OBERLEUTNANT SIGMUND STORP

SCALE
1 2 3 4 5 6 7 8 9 10 miles

B.A.Fansh 2

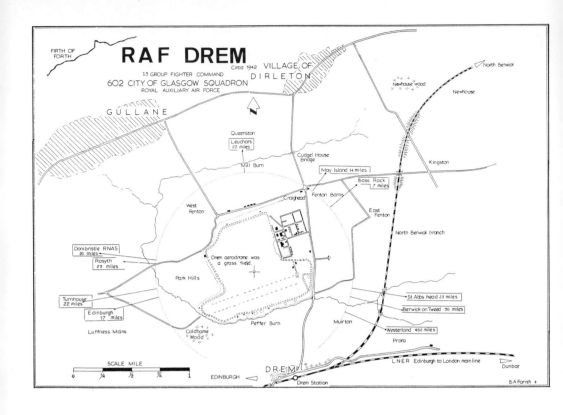

RAF DREM

Circa 1942

13 GROUP FIGHTER COMMAND

602 CITY OF GLASGOW SQUADRON
ROYAL AUXILIARY AIR FORCE

FIRTH OF FORTH

VILLAGE OF DIRLETON

GULLANE

Newhouse wood

North Berwick

Newhouse

Queenston

Leuchars 22 miles

Cudgel House Bridge

May Island 14 miles

Kingston

Mill Burn

Bass Rock 7 miles

Craighead

Fenton Barns

West Fenton

East Fenton

North Berwick branch

Donibristle RNAS 20 miles

Rosyth 23 miles

Drem aerodrome was a grass field.

Park Hills

St Abbs head 23 miles

Turnhouse 22 miles

Berwick on Tweed 30 miles

Edinburgh 17 miles

Muirton

Westerland 450 miles

Luffness Mains

Coldhame Wood

Peffer Burn

Prora

SCALE MILE

0   ¼   ½   ¾   1

EDINBURGH

D·R·E·M

Drem Station

L N E R Edinburgh to London main line

Dunbar

B A Farish 2

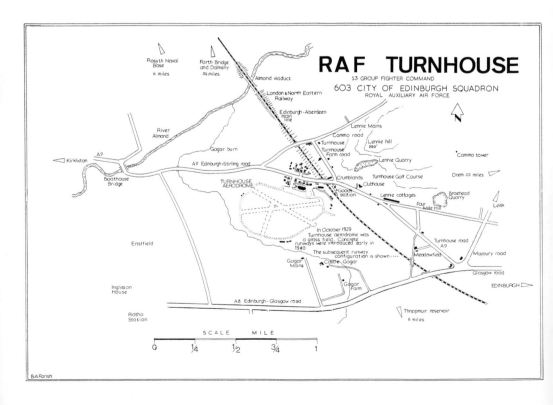

RAF TURNHOUSE

13 GROUP FIGHTER COMMAND

603 CITY OF EDINBURGH SQUADRON
ROYAL AUXILIARY AIR FORCE

Rosyth Naval Base
6 miles

Forth Bridge and Dalmeny
¾ miles

Almond viaduct

London & North Eastern Railway

River Almond

Edinburgh-Aberdeen main line

Lennie Mains

Cammo road

Lennie hill 250'

Cammo tower

Kirkliston

A9

Gogar burn

A9 Edinburgh-Stirling road

Turnhouse

Turnhouse Farm road

Lennie Quarry

Drem 22 miles

Boathouse Bridge

TURNHOUSE AERODROME

Crumblands

Clubhouse

Goods station

Turnhouse Golf Course

Lennie cottages

Braehead Quarry

Leith

Four Mile Hill

Eastfield

In October 1939 Turnhouse aerodrome was a grass field. Concrete runways were introduced early in 1940

Turnhouse road A9

Mayoury road

Gogar Mains

The subsequent runway configuration is shown ----

Castle Gogar

Meadowfield

Glasgow road

EDINBURGH

Ingliston House

Gogar Farm

Ratho Station

A8 Edinburgh-Glasgow road

Threipmuir reservoir
6 miles

SCALE   MILE

0   ¼   ½   ¾   1

B A Farish

fourth attempt he met O'Malley, who after a perfunctory examination and a bit of chitchat, passed him fit. Hugh Dundas was enlisted as a pupil pilot with 616 Squadron in May 1939.

One evening, while sitting by the fireplace in the officers' mess before dinner, Hugh Dundas came by his nickname, 'Cocky'. In fact, the name was given to him by a gentleman called Teddy St Aubyn. In need of refreshment, Teddy St Aubyn noticed that Hugh Dundas was suitably placed to ring the steward's bell.

'Hey you' he said. 'Hey you – Cocky – ring the bell.'

When asked why he had used the term Cocky, St Aubyn explained that he could not remember Hugh's name and that 'he looked like a bloody great Rhode Island Red'.

From his own book *Flying Start*, Hugh Dundas says of the Auxiliary Air Force:

'In all the history of arms there can seldom have been a body of men more outwardly confident and pleased with themselves than the pilots of the Auxiliary Air Force. We wore big brass "A"s on the lapels of our tunics and no amount of official pressure during the war would persuade us to remove them. The regulars insisted that those "A"s stood for 'Amateur Airmen', or even "Argue and Answer back". To us they were symbols of our membership of a very special club. Without the squadrons of the Auxiliary Air Force the Battle of Britain could not have been won. The pilots of the Auxiliary Air Force were lawyers and farmers, stock-brokers and journalists; they were landowners and artisans, serious-minded accountants and unrepentant playboys. They had two things in common – a passion for flying and a fierce determination that anything the regulars could do, the auxiliaries could do better. In order to implement this determination a very high standard of flying had to be achieved, as every auxiliary pilot secretly appreciated, in spite of the assumed contempt for regulars and all their ways. The auxiliary squadrons had been raised on a territorial basis. They were equipped with front-line aircraft, but most of them had training echelons so that pupil pilots could be put through their entire training within the unit. For this reason, the adjutant and assistant adjutant seconded to each squadron were invariably regular officers who had qualified as flying instructors at Central Flying School. Each squadron had a complement of Auxiliary Air Force ground crews and tradesmen, sufficient in number to service all the squadron's needs. But in addition there were about seventy-five Regular RAF ground staff, whose job it was not only to train the auxiliaries but also to keep the squadron aircraft in good working order throughout the week, when the auxiliaries were engaged in their normal civilian pursuits.'

Hugh Dundas began flying training in June 1939 with the Avro Tutor and in the same month was commissioned as Acting Pilot Officer. Soon after the declaration of war he received his Wings and was posted to No 2 Flying Training School at RAF Brize Norton, for an Advanced Training Course. However, by March 1940 he had rejoined 616 Squadron at Leconfield where he was to become aquainted with the Spitfire. In May 1940 the squadron was sent to Rochford to cover the evacuation from Dunkirk, where he had his first brush with the enemy on 28 May. On 3 July 1940 he made his first score which was a part share in a German bomber destroyed over an east coast convoy. During the famous *Adlertag* operations on 15 August, 616 Squadron intercepted a large force of Ju 88s near Bridlington and Hugh Dundas claimed one-and-a-half victories on that occasion. Three days after the squadron moved to Kenley on 19 August, Hugh Dundas was himself shot down, by an Me 109. For ten long days his injuries kept him firmly on the ground. His run of success really began after the squadron joined Douglas Bader's 12 Group 'Big Wing' in September 1940 and 'Tangmere Wing' in February 1941. On 8 May 1941 he was shot down for a second time by another Me 109 and crash landed near Hawkinge. In July he was promoted to Flight Lieutenant and took command of the squadron's A Flight, shortly to receive the Distinguished Flying Cross (DFC). On 21 September he was posted to No 59 Operational Training Unit, at Crosby-on-Eden as a Flight Commander, but returned to the auxiliary fold on 19 October when he was posted to 610 Squadron at Leconfield. On 20 December he took command of 56 Squadron at Duxford, and was promoted to Squadron Leader just as the unit was re-equipping with the Typhoon. In November 1942 while flying from Matlask, his Typhoon was badly damaged by flak off the Dutch coast. Managing to fly back across the channel he crash-landed at Coltishall. In mid-November he was posted to Duxford to form and lead the first Typhoon fighter-bomber Wing and was promoted to Acting Wing Commander.

In January 1943 Hugh Dundas was sent to Tunisia in North Africa as a Wing Leader, combining duties as supernumerary Wing Leader 324 Wing (Spitfires) and GTI Fighters 242 Group at Souk-el-Khemis. From Tunisia Hugh Dundas and his 324 Wing participated in the invasions of Sicily and Italy, and helped to cover the Salerno landings on 3 September.

In early 1944 he was posted to the RAF Staff College, at Haifa in Egypt. This proved to be a very short reprise from action, as a few days later his posting was cancelled and he was recalled to Italy to serve on AV-M Broadhurt's staff at AHQ Desert Air Force in place of an officer who had been killed in a flying accident. On 3 March 1944 he was awarded the Distinguished Service Order (DSO). On 31 May he took command of the five Spitfire squadrons in 244 Wing. The Wing provided close support for the Eighth Army during the battle for the Gothic Line and the subsequent advance. On 19 November he was promoted to Group Captain, and at only twenty-four years of age, he was the youngest Group Captain in the RAF at that time. Air Vice-Marshal David Scott-Malden, who had served with 603 Squadron himself told me: 'Cocky was seven months younger than me. I was born in December 1919. So we were both twenty-four in the latter half of 1944. However I was appointed Group Captain in charge of 125 Wing (4 Spitfire Squadrons) on 28 August 1944, and I have therefore always thought that, on appointment, I was the youngest Group Captain in the history of the RAF. Although after November, when we were both Group Captains aged twenty-four, Cocky was clearly the youngest in the RAF by seven months.' In March 1945, just prior to the final Eighth Army operations across the River Senio which led to the end of the war in Europe on 7 May, he was awarded the bar to his DSO. By this time he had accumulated eleven confirmed victories.

After the war from 1948 Hugh Dundas joined Beaverbrook Newspapers. In 1957 when he carried out most of the research for this book he was in London as Assistant General Manager of the Group comprising the *Daily Express, Sunday Express* and *Evening Standard,* including the *Scottish Daily Express* and *Sunday Express.* In 1961 he moved to the BET Group and became Managing Director in 1973 and Chairman in 1982. Between 1981 and 1987 he was the Chairman of Thames Television. Between 1947 and 1950 he was once again reunited with his oldest love, the Royal Auxiliary Air Force. This time he was in Command of 601 (County of London) Squadron. Consequently, when the flying squadrons of the Royal Auxiliary Air Force were disbanded in 1957, the voice of Hugh Dundas was added to the file of champions, dedicated to its survival.

So, as you can no doubt appreciate I felt pretty confident of securing some element of help from Sir Hugh, when writing a project about the Royal Auxiliary Air Force. I at once sent him a sample copy of my book *Forewarned is Forearmed* and a begging letter. A short while later I received a favourable reply, not only promising to think over the question in hand, but also making some very commendatory remarks regarding my little tome (says I with pride).

Hardly could I guess, at this point in time, the wonderful gift which was to be entrusted to me. Serendipity, is the accidental discovery of good fortune. A term coined by Horace Walpole in 1754. It must be like stumbling into the elephant's graveyard, King Solomon's mines, or the resting place of the Holy Grail whilst out on a Sunday stroll. If you don't believe in such things, then the rest of this story may lose a little of its magic. I have lived with a firm trust in two things; a belief in destiny and a belief in myself. These two forces inevitably create a cocktail for success. This may not happen immediately, you may have numerous failures, of which I am living proof. But if you never stop believing, then one day, Horace Walpole was right, serendipity will spring out of nowhere, like a demented kangaroo.

I remember the day in question very well; Saturday 16 January 1994. I had just arrived home from RAF Lyneham where I had spent the day on a 'Conduct After Capture' course, overseen by the RAF Regiment Flight. My two children, Jason aged six and Emily aged four, were running around the house in typically boistrous form.

The telephone rang, which I answered while covering my left ear with the palm of my hand to diminish the sound of the children, who had by now, somehow managed to get hold of two of my golf clubs and were enthusiastically putting a ball around the utility room in a shrieking frenzy.

I announced who I was, and a deep, powerful voice announced who he was. 'This is Hugh Dundas!' At that point the conversation came to an abrupt halt. It wouldn't be an exaggeration to say that I was dumbstruck. I suppose an immediate reaction suggested that this was a practical joke. But how could it be? Then it suddenly dawned on me that I was actually talking to Sir Hugh Dundas. On grasping that reality, try and imagine how I felt. On the other end of the telephone was one of my boyhood heroes; one of 'The Few'! It must be a similar feeling to a film buff being telephoned by their favourite movie star, or a music lover being called up by their favourite artiste.

Eventually, with all the finesse of an American disc jockey, I replied, 'Hi! Sir Hugh!'

Confused by the lengthy silence, and I can only assume, bemused by the screaming of children, he said: 'If this isn't a good time I could ring back later.'

'No! No!' I insisted. After all, if I let him put the telephone down now after such an embarrassing introduction, he might not be inclined to wish to repeat the experience. I quickly explained that my wife was just about to take the children up for their bath, which she did, leaving the room in silence. Sir Hugh explained to me that after I had written to him about the auxiliary history, it had got him thinking. His memory was plunged back to 1957, which was a very important year in auxiliary terms, because in that year the Royal Auxiliary Air Force, was disbanded (it was also the year that I was born). All of the flying squadrons along with many supporting units were systematically run down. When this happened Sir Hugh explained that he himself had toyed with the idea of writing an auxiliary history. He had done a fair amount of research but had never managed to get anything finished. His notes remained in the same folder which had been their home for thirty-five years. He then said: 'Perhaps you would like them? You might find them useful?' He was just about to go away for a short period and he promised that on Monday morning he would put the whole bundle in the post to me, with the instruction, 'You can do what you like with it'.

At this point I still didn't expect anything other than just a few notes, which may prove to be of some help in my research. Needless to say, the expectancy of the next few days was addictive. Sir Hugh had kept his word, and on returning home from work on Tuesday there was a large brown envelope waiting for me.

That evening I sat down to try and see what exactly I had. I was presented with a folder full of letters. Some were carbons of the letters which Sir Hugh had sent himself, others were their replies. There was a chapter synopsis for the first chapter of an unfinished book. There were letters to and from Collins, the publishers, about his ideas. And there were a number of photographs and even negatives in their original packets.

The more I looked, the more I began to understand the importance of this work. There were letters to Dundas from the House of Commons, the Air Ministry, South Africa and Germany. But who were all these people? The more I delved, the more the pieces in the puzzle began to come together in my own mind. The chapter synopsis and most of the finished text concerned 16 October 1939; the first Nazi air raid on mainland Britain and the men who flew on that day. Some of the letters seemed to have come from airmen who had actually taken part in the fighting that day, whom Dundas had tracked down in 1957. There were tantilising clues concerning dinner engagements and meetings at the Kennel Club. It became clear that Dundas was very well-known within the circles that his research was taking him. Most of the letters began with, 'Dear Cocky!' or 'My dearest Cocky!'.

The more I read, the more I became involved with these men, with their stories and their participation on that historic day, or in the events leading up to it. The research was so thorough and now by some miracle of fate, its future had been placed into my loving hands. I felt like a literary Indiana Jones, who had uncovered a wonderful treasure, lost to the world for many years.

I read on into the small hours of the morning, hypnotised. I knew at once that this was something special and that the contents of the brown folder would be wasted on the book I was already compiling on the RAuxAF. Because of the enormity of the subject, I could only warrant few words on such an event.

The idea came to me almost immediately, that here I had been given the chance to write a second book. A book that would ultimately focus on that day in October, but would hint at the years of research; the succession of events, all linked together, as if by some divine guiding hand. These events go back even further than 1939, to 1924, when the Auxiliary Air Force was first formed. To understand the magic of that October day, you have to appreciate what the Auxiliary Air Force was all about, and the kind of men who served in its ranks. This I discovered, had been Sir Hugh's own ambition when he set about writing the history himself. Sir Hugh's intention was not to write a formal history about the Auxiliary Air Force, but rather to produce a book which would be readable to the general public and which would reflect the unique spirit and flavour of the auxiliary squadrons, whose motto is 'We accompany them to the stars'.

What follows draws heavily upon the research concealed within Sir Hugh's brown folder. Some sections of text are indeed lightly edited versions of his own writings, which may to some extent, help to explain the often disjointed style. The other main source of information has come from the people who were actually there on the day the raid took place. The importance of this story, is not just the relevance of a great historical event, but also a look at the way in which those people were introduced to the Second World War on the Home Front. This is their story, largely re-told in their own words. At the beginning of the book, a list acknowledges those who have helped in some way, but there are one or two people who deserve particular thanks. First of these is the writer Andrew Jeffrey. Andrew is himself an authority on the Forth Raid, and has written several articles on the subject, as well as dedicating a chapter to it in his book *This Present Emergency*. Several years of painstaking research were kindly made available to me. The next person is Brian Farish, whose father Alex worked for the L.N.E.R., and was present during the raid. Because of this family connection, Brian has always had his own interest in the subject, and has done some important research himself. Chapter three of the book *Target Rosyth*, which studies the events which led up to the Forth Raid, is written

almost entirely in his own words. Group Captain Sir Hugh Dundas and
– thirty-six years later – Henry Buckton, have merely been a combined
pen for all these voices.

Henry Buckton

I ONLY CAME IN FOR THE DANCING!

onday 16 October 1939, dawned fair and cloudy. Visibility not bad, with slight ground haze and broken cloud over land. Clear sky lanes in between at about 4,000 feet. This was the Phoney War, a time for men to wait. By now the war was into its second month. It was unlikely that anybody waking up that day in or around the capital would have conceivably imagined what was about to happen. After all, if the war did come to Britain, it would come to the south; to London. Edinburgh it would seem was too distant from the European airfields to make it a probable target; at least at this stage. There are many contradictions and mixed feelings about the events of 16 October, but the one area in which everybody is in agreement, is that the weather was fair.

The ground on which the airfield at Drem was built was owned by Dr Chalmers Watson, who was accredited with producing the very first herd of TT-test milk cows in Britain. His wife was the former actress Lily Brayton, who had played the leading role in *Chu Chin Chow*, on the London stage during the First World War. The couple lived in a large house nearby. Drem itself was precariously balanced on the top of a hill, some two miles south of Gullane, which nestles on the south shore of the Firth of Forth, seventeen miles east of Edinburgh. I say precarious because many – even some of the more experienced pilots – had trouble landing down the hill, often ending up in a marshy area at its base; from where they had to be rescued. Before vacating the airfield prior to 602 Squadron's arrival on Friday 13 October, No 13 Flying Training School had occupied a number of wooden huts, which were to make ideal dispersal sites for the Glasgow squadron who apparently had the place completely to themselves.

At 9a.m. on 16 October 1939, B Flight of 602 Squadron, led by Flight Lieutenant George Pinkerton, came on duty. They went to the

Flight Hut to wait for patrol orders. Not a very luxurious place, some chairs, a stove in the middle with a rickety chimney, some pin-ups and identification charts on the wall.

The readiness section – George Pinkerton, Flying Officer Archie McKellar, and Flying Officer Paul Webb – went over to the Watch Hut, where Flight Lieutenant Cairns Smith, thirty-nine-year-old veteran of the First World War and a printer in Kilmarnock, was Flying Control Officer. To the squadron he was known as Mrs Cairns for his fastidious attempts to keep the floor clear of cigarette ends and for his unflagging aptitude for making tea. He sat facing the runways at a window of the Watch Hut, a telephone at his elbow to receive orders from the Ops room at Turnhouse, twenty-two miles to the west.

The RAF squadrons employed various states of readiness, the most relaxed of which was 'released'. If a flight was released then its time was very much its own, since it was not expected to be in operation until a specified hour. In the meantime, the personnel could undertake routine maintenance or training flights, or play games and generally relax. If it was known for certain how long the release period would last, they would even be allowed to leave the station. The next state was 'available', which meant that the squadron members must be ready to spring into action, fully-equipped and prepared. 'Readiness' was a similar state, but pilots were given a certain time-scale in which they would have to be airborne – normally a matter of minutes – and all personnel concerned had to stay close to their aircraft. 'Readiness' was the state in which George Pinkerton and B Section of 602 Squadron found themselves that morning, with no emergency or intimation of what was about to unfold. There were still greater degrees of readiness. During 'stand-by', pilots actually had to sit in their aircraft, with the engine switched off, but ready to take off immediately on receiving instructions from the sector controller.

602 (City of Glasgow) Squadron was one of the very first Auxiliary Air Force units to be formed. This event took place on 12 September 1925 at Renfrew, where they were destined to remain for the next eight years. During that time the squadron was equipped with a number of different aircraft: Airco DH 9A, they received in October 1925; Fawn in September 1927 and Wapiti in July 1929. 602 was one of only two auxiliary units to receive the Fairey Fawn, the other being 503.

The DH 9A aircraft had been used in France towards the end of the First World War as part of the Independent Bombing Force in raids over Germany. The Fairey Fawn was the first of the post-war generation of light day-bombers to enter service with the RAF, first introduced in 1924 and remaining in service until 1929. The Westland Wapiti first became available to the RAF in 1928, remaining in service until 1939. The Wapiti found its way into the hangars of many auxiliary squadrons and proved to be extremely strong and reliable, as well as fully aerobatic. The Wapiti's reputation was enhanced by its active service on the North-West Frontier of India and Iraq. Here it was used on army co-operation duties as a day bomber.

On 20 January 1933, 602 Squadron moved to Abbotsinch a few miles to the west where they happily remained for a further six years. While at Abbotsinch the squadron was equipped with Hart in February 1934; Hind in June 1936; Hector in November 1938; Gauntlet II in January 1939; and Spitfire I in May 1939.

The Hawker Hector entered service in May 1937 and was intended principally for army co-operation. The Hawker Hind was issued to a total of fourteen squadrons of the AAF and Special Reserve, which was more than any other aircraft; it was the last biplane light-bomber to be used by the RAF and was a development of the Hawker Hart with a more powerful engine.

To emphasise the exclusive nature of the auxiliary units, a young man wishing to join 602 Squadron had to undergo a series of discreet tests. These tests were designed to determine the candidates social acceptability. Some of these young men even owned their own planes; which would naturally have been a bonus in their favour. The final test for entry into 602 was a dining-in night, designed to see how much alcohol these well-bred young men could consume, and how they conducted themselves afterwards. As the war years rolled on, this golden image began to tarnish. After all, the country was soon going to run out of eligible playboys. The serious business of flying and war brought heavy casualties to many of the auxiliary units and non-auxiliary personnel were brought in as replacements. Regular officers and auxiliaries were soon to be flying into battle side by side. However, the regulars remained a little cautious of the auxiliaries in these squadrons, particularly when it came to socialising. Going for a drink could be an expensive affair as the more prestigious auxiliaries invariably insisted on champagne. Our story only takes us up to 16 October 1939, at which time the golden image was firmly intact (thank heavens); which is undoubtedly one of the reasons why their success on that day must have seemed so magical at the time. These were the amateurs putting the professionals to shame. These were the long-haired layabouts, sneered at by regular officers as time-wasters.

If the Auxiliary Air Force felt in competition with the RAF, there was also rivalry within the ranks of the service itself, especially between the Scottish auxiliaries and the Sassenachs below the border; in particular the glamour boys from Hendon who always seemed to have the public eye. Auxiliary squadrons, as we have already established, were generally made up of reasonably well-off young men. At weekends they enjoyed flying as a hobby and in some ways a privilege of their class: although others took the whole thing far more seriously of course. The squadrons had become their own exclusive clubs. 601 (County of London) Squadron which became nicknamed the 'millionaire's squadron', certainly lived up to its title, pushing rivalry to the limits when petrol rationing was introduced. In order to keep their cars on the road, they had a whip-round and purchased their very own petrol station.

Marcus Robinson who was a Flight Lieutenant with 602 Squadron on the day of the Forth Raid, claims there was no rivalry between the Scottish Auxiliaries themselves. 'We were very good friends, and in February 1935, a rugby match was organised between the Glasgow and Edinburgh Squadrons on one side, and two of the English Squadrons on the other side; which would take place at Usworth near Newcastle. We set off in our Harts with Douglas Farquhar leading, and before long we were caught up in the middle of a blinding snow storm.' In their attempt to get home, the pilots became separated and the whole unfortunate episode ended with aircraft strewn across the Lothians; two completely written off and four others severely damaged. Robinson himself came down in the middle of a boggy field and Douglas Farquhar ended up on the beach at Portobello. Farquhar was convinced that he was going to be court-martialled. He wasn't – but rugby was a dirty word at the Air Ministry for some time afterwards. Marcus Robinson was also the very first man to land an aircraft on the Isle of Arran. His family had a house on the island and he decided to pay them a visit in an Avro 504, which the squadron used as a trainer. He was extremely pleased with this achievement, until a local farmer said he owed him five shillings for terrifying his sheep.

On 16 October 1939, Dunlop Urie, who today lives in New South Wales, Australia, would lead Yellow Section of A Flight against the Forth Raiders. His pre-war experiences as an auxiliary pilot were most likely very similar to those of the other pilots on the squadron at the time.

'I joined 602 Squadron at Abbotsinch near Glasgow in April 1935 when I was nineteen years old. My first flight was with Lord Clydesdale our CO. My instruction started on 15 April with Flight Lieutenant Mark Selway. My first solo was on 26 May on an Avro 504 when I had done twelve hours dual instruction. The Avro 504 was a relic of the First World War when it had been a Fighter aircraft. In September 1935 I started getting dual instruction on a Hart, the operational bomber with which the Squadron was equipped. After two hours' dual I went solo in October 1935. I was awarded my 'Wings' in March 1936 after a total of 20 hours dual and 65 hours solo. In June 1936 we converted from Harts to Hinds. The Hind was similar to the Hart but with a supercharged engine.

'In 1938 came the Munich Crisis. I was sitting my Finals for a B.Sc. degree in Applied Chemistry, but only got 2nd Class Honours as we were very involved with the crisis. After this we were converted from Bombers to Army Co-operation and equipped with Hectors in November 1938. I had done a total of 450 hours' flying by then. In January 1939 we were converted once again, this time to Fighters, and equipped with Gauntlets.

'In May 1939 it was decided to equip us with Spitfires and we were given a Fairey Battle to convert us to low-wing monoplanes. After flying the Battle for one hour I did my first flight on a Spitfire on 18 May 1939. I still think that flight was the most thrilling experience of my life. The aircraft was so absolutely "RIGHT". It was a big change from the Gauntlet: retractable undercarriage, flaps, variable pitch prop, cruising at 240 mph instead of 120. In August 1939 we were mobilised, by which time I had done twenty-five hours on Spitfires.

'On mobilisation we dispersed our aircraft at the edge of the airfield at Abbotsinch and pitched tents beside them. Three of the pilots, Finlay Boyd, Donald Jack and myself were engaged to be married when we were mobilised. We were all anxious to get married as soon as possible. It was arranged that we should each be given twenty-four hours leave to do so. Donald was married on 7 September, Mary and I on 8 September and Finlay on 9 September. We were married in our church in Glasgow and went to Aberfoyle for our honeymoon. On our way back we bought a caravan and parked it near our Dispersal Point at Abbotsinch and so started our married life, which has lasted more than fifty-six years so far. On 13 October 1939 we were moved to Drem. At this time I had been promoted to Flight Lieutenant and was leading Yellow Section of A Flight.'

On 16 October 1939, Flight Lieutenant George Pinkerton, aided by Flying Officer Archie McKellar, would shoot down the Ju 88 flown by *Hauptmann* Helmut Pohle. Pinkerton was thirty years old, a quiet, solid, steady, meticulous sort of chap – so solid and steady that he was nick-named 'Grouchy' (later changed to 'Grumpy' when the squadron pilots named themselves after the seven dwarfs). Two months previously, he had been a fruit-farmer at Houston, near Paisley, in Renfrewshire. He had been married for eighteen months, and had a daughter six months old. But for all his solid respectability, Pinkerton had always had a craving for speed. Soon after he left school, he became a professional dirt-track rider, and only stopped that after two years because of stiff maternal opposition. He used his earnings to learn to fly; each weekend he went out to nearby Abbotsinch airfield, and for £2 an hour he was taught to handle Moths. When this became too expensive, he joined 602 Squadron in 1931, and learned to fly in Avro 504 Ns, Hawker Hinds and Harts (learning to be a bomber pilot), Hectors, and Gauntlets. In May 1939 the squadron switched to Spitfires – the first auxiliary unit to be fitted with them. And just to keep up the pace on land, he owned a fast Alvis. Right up until a couple of years before he died, George Pinkerton could regularly be seen whizzing around his Scottish farm on a small Honda motorcycle.

Pinkerton was mobilised in August 1939. By that time he had already flown about 1,000 hours, civil and air force. From the day of his mobilisation, he seldom saw his wife, although his farm was only six minutes from the airfield. On Friday 13 October, Flight Lieutenant George Pinkerton and the thirteen Spitfires of 602 Squadron roared off into the darkness of 6.50a.m. At 7.15a.m., they touched down at Drem in East Lothian, to take up position at the forward base in the Turnhouse Sector of 13 Group, Fighter Command. The squadron spent the weekend settling down; little expecting, or preparing for what was about to happen.

George Pinkerton survived the war and returned to his fruit-farm at Houston, having been promoted to Group Captain and awarded the OBE and DFC. He died in 1993.

Little Archie McKellar, the plasterer's apprentice from Paisley, was twenty-seven years old and only five-foot-three when he was called up as a Flying Officer in August 1939. He was the sort of man, according to his colleagues, who was bound to get himself killed. They called him the pocket Hercules, because of his passion for physical fitness. He was immensely cheerful, aggressively voluble, and a complete dare-devil. He had joined 602 in 1936 against his father's wishes, after saving up his apprentice's pay in his father's business to learn to fly in secret. On hearing of the outbreak of war he was heard to say 'Christ, I didn't join up to fight – I only came in for the dancing!'

McKellar was killed on 1 November 1940. By that time he had a string of medals, and was the Squadron Leader of 605 Hurricane Squadron near London. He had twenty kills to his credit, and had become a legend, a symbol of Glasgow toughness. Once he shot down three planes in three seconds, with the same burst, in a head-on attack against a force of Heinkels. Once he chopped a plane a day for eight successive days. Archie McKellar and George Pinkerton between them were credited with the shooting down of *Hauptmann* Helmut Pohle's Ju 88 off May Island on 16 October 1939. Twelve days later on 28 October, he played the main part in shooting down the first enemy aircraft to crash on the British mainland during the Second World War – a Heinkel He 111 on a hill near Haddington, in East Lothian (Patsy Gifford of 603 Squadron had a hand in this one too). On another occasion, less creditably perhaps, he wrenched his Spitfire out of an upside-down dive-cum-roll so forcibly that he gave its wings a permanent wave. Every rivet was bent.

The third member of Pinkerton's section on 16 October was Paul Webb, who, at a critical moment during the day ahead, sheered off on a pursuit of his own. He missed out in the destruction of Pohle, but achieved a successful career with the RAF, which led to the rank of Air Commodore. The three men were great friends and Paul Webb who lives in Wales today, recalls: 'I was No 3 with George Pinkerton and Archie McKellar on many occasions before and during the war. At various times we flew Hinds, Gauntlets and Spitfires together.'

Shortly after 9a.m. on the 16 October, Flight Lieutenant Cairns Smith (Mrs Cairns) the Flying Control Officer at Drem, reported that Villa Blue (Blue Section of 602) was at readiness; and at 9.45a.m., the section was ordered to patrol May Island at Angels Five (5,000 feet) to investigate unidentified aircraft. At 9.20am the Chain Home radar station at Drone Hill near St Abb's Head on the east coast of Scotland, had detected aircraft approaching from across the North Sea. Unknown to them, these aircraft were two Heinkel He 111s, which had set out from their base at Westerland on the Island of Sylt, to carry out a pre-raid reconnaissance of the area.

At last, the three Spitfires flown by Pinkerton, McKellar and Webb were in the air. The Spitfire I with which both 602 and 603 Squadrons were equipped had a maximum speed of 346 mph and could cruise quite happily at 240 mph as Dunlop Urie points out, although a cruising speed of 304 mph was quite attainable. Its recommended ceiling was 30,500 feet, and it had a range of 415 miles, which took into consideration 15 minutes for its take-off and climb. By reducing this cruising speed to 175 mph, its range could be extended to 600 miles. As the auxiliary units within Fighter Command at the time were employed in a defensive role around the British Isles, this should have been ample for most operational purposes: unless pilots decided to wander too far over the sea, which as you will discover later, caused a few problems on the day for Green Section of A Flight.

At 9.45a.m. a German aircraft was spotted over Dunfermline at high altitude, by an Observer Corps Post of 36 Group, and appeared to be heading towards the Royal Navy base at Rosyth. Another aircraft was spotted and tracked by Observer Corps posts belonging to 31 Group, Galashiels. Both of these aircraft were identified by the Observer Corps as Heinkel He 111s. At 10.08a.m. one of these aircraft was noticed by lookouts onboard HMS *Edinburgh*, which lay anchored just east of the Forth railway bridge. Visibility was fair, and the Heinkel crew had established the location of several Royal Navy ships. At this point with its mission accomplished, the Heinkel turned for home, and began to fly east towards the coast. It was observed over Drem at 10.11a.m.

At 9.49a.m. Drone Hill radar station broke down. This has traditionally been put down to a total power failure and was just the first of many problems which frustrated and impeded the RAF throughout the day. 'Radar' (Radio Detection and Ranging) was an American word. The English system was originally known as RDF (Radio Direction-Finding) or, later 'radio location', and the word 'radar' was not adopted by the Royal Air Force until 1943. Thus, on 16 October 1939, the correct terminology we should adopt is RDF. However, in the interest of not trying to confuse the reader, and at the risk of being termed 'politically incorrect' by the purists, we shall call the system employed that day, 'radar'. By the start of the Second World War, a number of radar stations had been built around the coast, stretching from Southampton to the Forth. This network was known as Chain Home.

The failure at Drone Hill was not due to the loss of the public electricity supply (as stated in 13 Group ORB). It was in fact due to the failure of an amplifier valve. More specifically, an amplifier valve began sparking internally at 4.07p.m. on 15 October and this caused the transmitter to fail. The problem was compounded by the failure of another valve and the fact that Drone Hill did not have a stock of spare NT57 valves. Two spare valves were sent from Driffield Section Maintenance Depot and arrived at 10.30a.m. on 16 October. In the meantime however, Drone Hill had managed (at 11.59p.m. on the 15th) to get back on the air at much reduced power. The station went off air again at 09.35a.m., and went back on at reduced power within half an hour. It then went out of service at 12.25p.m. as the new valves were fitted. The station was reported operating at 15 kilowatts (giving a range of about 60 miles) by 12.45p.m., but does not appear to have been fully operational until 3.55p.m.

Flight Lieutenant George Pinkerton and the rest of Blue Section duly arrived at their patrol point, the Isle of May. This was a remote offshore island at the mouth of the Firth of Forth, which presented the most likely approach towards Edinburgh for the enemy. Some twelve miles north of Dunbar and six miles south of Crail, this was an inhospitable windswept rock, which through the presence of an anti-aircraft battery, kept watch over the mouth of the Forth like a geological sentinel.

Twenty minutes after arriving, George Pinkerton was ordered to turn south and make for the coast at Dunbar. There was obviously something brewing. It soon became evident that the speck in the distance was an intruder. At 10.15a.m., he intercepted an enemy aircraft. He ordered his section into line astern for No 1 attack. The enemy plane turned 45 degrees to port and dived for cloud. Pinkerton fired 720 rounds from his eight .303 Browning machine-guns at very long range. Archie McKellar spent a further 1,000 rounds. Paul Webb, Blue 3, was unable to get any rounds off.

These 1,720 rounds were the first shots to be fired during air fighting over the British Isles during the Second World War. This was also the very first occasion on which Spitfires had been engaged against an enemy in combat. Pinkerton noted in his log-book: 'This was the first interception to be made over this country of an enemy aircraft; unfortunately unsuccessful'.

Blue Section landed at Drem again at 10.44a.m. Meanwhile other sections had taken off and chased around without success. Both sections of A Flight had operated search patrols, and both had reported an above average level of R/T chatter. It was almost like a premonition of something about to happen. Sandy Johnstone of Green Section had felt it, and Marcus Robinson of Red Section felt in his bones that 'something was afoot.'

At 11a.m. Green Section of A Flight was ordered to take-off and proceed to May Island. The section consisted of Squadron Leader Douglas Farquhar, Flight Lieutenant Sandy Johnstone and Flying Officer Ian Ferguson.

On 16 October 1939 Douglas Farquhar was the CO of 602 Squadron. He survived the war and in 1957 Hugh Dundas had managed to track him down. He was by then a director of Karino Farms (Pty) Limited, Transvaal, South Africa. From his own log-books he was able to compose many interesting pre-war events which were related to Hugh Dundas in a letter dated 4 April 1957. I have included them to give a brief outline of the squadron and the type of men who were flying that day.

'The AAF squadrons were originally equipped with the DH 9A but Renfrew was a very small aerodrome and we were re-equipped with the Fairey Fawn in October 1927. One of these machines arrived and was on the tarmac when I came down one weekend and I was asked if I would like a trip in the back. On landing and being asked what I thought of it I replied that it really must have been hell when one had to fly such things. The pilot's face was a study when he blurted out "Had to fly such things, why you are going to be re-equipped with them!"

'The AAF were invited to enter crews for the Armament Officers' Bombing Trophy which was competed for at North Coates Fitties in October 1930. The competition was open to all day-bomber squadrons. 601 and 602 entered and I piloted for the latter. There was considerable surprise when 602 was placed second, being only beaten by 12 Squadron which was then considered the crack day-bomber squadron. We flew Wapitis and the official report commented on our bad luck in having a hang-up and an accidental release due to unsatisfactory release gear on the Wapiti. This has been very strongly reported upon to the Air Ministry. One hates to think what would have happened had we had no trouble and won the competitions; as it was the AAF were not again invited (so far as I know)! In November 1929 (then) Sir Hugh Trenchard had presented the Esher Trophy to us and in his speech had said "I look forward to the day when the Auxiliary Air Force will be as efficient as the Royal Air Force." He didn't have so long to wait.

'In 1934 we had Harts and had a craze for stopping our engines and gliding around from 8,000 or so down to 2,000 feet and re-starting by diving. The craze dies when someone – I think David McIntyre – failed to restart. I have some excellent photographs of myself with prop stopped; rather unusual.

'In 1935 we sent a detachment to the Royal Review at Mildenhall. We stood proudly in front of our highly polished Harts as H.M. drove down the line. Deflation was instantaneous as we heard the Air Super Marshal remark "This is the Birmingham Squadron, Sir." 602 were the first auxiliaries to go to an armament practice camp when we spent our annual camp at N. Coates Fitties in July 1935. I kept some of the messages that air-gunners handed to me in the days before satisfactory intercom. Here are three examples: (a) Message from me to gunner "Wind in aerial" reply from AG "Aerial was never out." (This on a WT exercise!) (b) "Too much static electricity in the air sir, have reeled in. P.S. GOT SHOCK." (c) "Base ask for our position. I would save you the trouble sir but I am not familiar with the countryside."

'In – I think – May 1934 there was a lunch party at a private aerodrome in Yorkshire to which all AAF squadrons sent flights. I think it was laid on by Jackie Baldwin. I led the 602 flight and we were absolutely on the dot. Instructions were to land and taxi to a parking area marked by a white flag. Our landing was delayed by the fact that a young gentleman from Hendon had finished up on his nose and tempers were, unknown to me, frayed. On landing we turned smartly into line astern and I moved towards the white flag. Immediately it was waved violently so I stopped, whereupon it was held steady. I started to taxi forward whereupon the flag was waved violently. This went on for some time until I told my passenger to run over and find out the form. He returned at high speed with a red face and the message "obey orders and taxi to the white flag". I then did this and an irate W/C was extremely informal. I replied, "The orders never mentioned a flag being waved and if he had held the bloody thing steady I should have continued what I was already doing, namely to taxi towards it." It was only four years later that I learnt that I should have become CO of 602 a year earlier had there not been this black mark against me. So the moral is that auxiliaries could not always argue and answer back and get away with it!

'602 got overkeen on night flying from October 1937. The solution to the large number of night hours we put in probably lies in the convenient site of Abbotsinch aerodrome. (In my own case midway between office and home). We received our first Spitfires in mid-May 1939 and started night-flying on them in mid-August. We had cause to regret our keenness when the war started and we were the only fighters operational both day and night north of the Humber. We had aircraft at readiness or available night and day for many weeks without a break and this was only modified when an accident occurred which I attributed to the pilot being over-tired and was able to prove that with our numbers of pilots adequate rest was impossible.'

Farquhar goes on to explain in another letter to Hugh Dundas:

'There is one point about which I feel somewhat bitter and a paragraph could put things right. After the Forth Bridge show on 16 October 1939 our AOC specially warned us that we should be on our toes in case a revenge bomber attack was delivered on Drem. Owing to our night and day commitments it was never possible to practise squadron scrambles but I had laid down very carefully drawn orders based on the assumption that I should lead. (This was a safe assumption as I would know if the whole squadron was brought to readiness.) By a stroke of ill-luck I was detailed to sit on a court martial at Turnhouse a few days later when the squadron was ordered off and vectored onto bandits (not bogeys). They turned out to be Hampdens returning from Norway (I think) and they were under the impression that they were flying into the Cromarty Firth. They had no IFF on, were not in line astern, had their undercarts up, were nipping through cloud and fired the wrong colours. In spite of all this the leader of 602 recognised them as Hampdens as he went in to attack and pulled away. His radio call (no VHF at that time) was not heard by all and to cut a long story short, fire was opened by one or possibly two pilots and two Hampdens were shot down. When I got back from the court martial (a Cpl charged with stealing a 10/-note!) Batchy had already arrived for the court of enquiry – which eventually exonerated 602. When I heard the whole horrid story I expressed some surprise that the armoured Hampdens had been shot down so easily. The whole episode got twisted until the story became generally accepted that I was leading the squadron, and remarked after that, anyhow, it was good shooting practice or words to that effect. I only learnt this in early 1941 when I had reason to pick up a friend at Coningsby mess. After we left he said, "I hope you didn't mind the coolness in the atmosphere," and when I asked him what he meant I heard the story. Years after it was still going strong and I gave up chasing it. Later on one of our pilots on convoy escort was vectored onto a bandit "shadowing the convoy" and fired a short burst before recognising it as an Anson with the new marking roundels about which we knew nothing. As a result he had done no night-flying and his colour blindness had not been noticed. He was exonerated on this ground. As a result of these two events we got the evil reputation of being trigger happy and it is even mentioned in Guy Gibson's book.

'It is an old story that I tried to land near a Heinkel that I had shot down and turned upside down as a result of a soft patch. What is not appreciated is that this was the first enemy aircraft to be attacked by cannon fire and I felt it was of considerable importance to get the evidence of what – if anything – had happened. As leader it was my job to knock out the rear gunner whereupon my No 2 was supposed to go in close and blow the thing to bits with cannon. I had seen my No 2 firing but he had dived away and would not answer on the R/T. (It turned out he went in too fast and blacked out as he broke away.) The German crew carried the gunner to the protection of a stone wall which made it obvious that they were going to destroy their aircraft and it seemed to me that there was a good chance of stopping them by landing in what seemed a good stubble field. I might mention that the German pilot wrote to me and we had quite a correspondence towards the end of the war. The troops who eventually turned up thought I was a Hun too and it was a bit trying to be first the prisoner of the Germans and then of a friendly search-light unit! I got a real raspberry from Group into the bargain and generally felt misunderstood! By the way, the cannon pilot was Proudman and attached to us for this special duty. He was killed during the Battle of Britain and I was told that he found a string of 110s doing the defensive circle trick so went inside the circle in the opposite direction with the sad result mentioned.'

Sandy Johnstone who also flew with Green Section on 16 October 1939, later became CO of 602 himself. In fact he was to command the unit through one of its most crucial periods; the Battle of Britain. Like Farquhar he had joined the squadron before the war. About three months before the outbreak he had been appointed to run the Volunteer Reserve Section of the Civil Air Navigation School at Prestwick. He had also been a previous employee of Scottish Aviation Ltd during its construction of the airfield at Grangemouth; which had been a possible forward operating base for 602 Squadron, as Drem was still under the control of Flying Training Command. With his friend Sandy Mackay who was the manager of a branch of his family's bakery business in the little town of Largs, to the west of Glasgow, he enjoyed sailing around the Cumbraes as a pre-war pleasure and perhaps necessary distraction from the serious business in the offing. Just before the war the unit was based at Abbotsinch, from where Johnstone was to shuttle to and fro in his Vauxhall; with trips to see his parents and fiancée Margaret in Glasgow. Shortly after the issue of gas-masks the 602 pilots were able to daub what Johnstone described as 'puke green' blobs of gas-detecting paint on their treasured vehicles: the Vauxhall annointed thus on the bonnet. When 602 Squadron arrived at Drem on Friday 13 October 1939, a superstitious person would no doubt have suspected failure, rather than jubilant success on the following Monday. After all – as Sandy Johnstone noticed – not only was it Friday 13, but 13 people sat down to breakfast before flying 13 aircraft to Drem, the home of No 13 Flying Training School; where they would operate as a unit within No 13 Group Fighter Command. Yes indeed, that superstitious person may well have doubted the outcome of the approaching fray; had of course they not been able to predict its inevitability. On the day the squadron arrived at Drem, Sandy Johnstone was one of the pilots who – if you remember I mentioned earlier – had difficulty encountering the down-hill gradient; becoming the first of many to squelch into the perfectly placed quagmire.

The third member of Green Section was Flying Officer Ian Ferguson. One story about Ferguson always sticks in my mind as a sort of testimonial to his character. On 18 August 1940, the day which was considered by many to have been the hardest fought day of the entire Battle of Britain, 602 Squadron was based at Westhampnett near Portsmouth. This was the first time that the pilots had been able to rest for five days, as they had spent up to sixteen hours of each of those days at readiness. It also gave the groundcrew a rare chance to carry out essential maintenance work on the squadron's aircraft. This release was to be short-lived and when the scramble was given, many of those aircraft were up on jacks, having their wheels changed. Eventually, the squadron became airborne and patrolled at 20,000 feet above Tangmere, until Stukas were spied attacking the airfield at Ford. Flying Officer Ian Ferguson was pursuing one of the Stukas when he was pounced upon by a Messerschmitt Bf 109E. Damaged by the German's cannon shells, he was forced to make for home. Intending to crash-land his aircraft, he suddenly became aware that he was heading straight for

Littlehampton. Instead of baling out of the aircraft he decided to stay with it until it was out of harm's way. Just north of the town he thundered through some overhead power lines. His propeller sliced through four of the 33,000 volt conductors. Littlehampton found itself without electricity for some time and Ferguson managed to crash-land safely near Toddington. Ian Ferguson is one of the least remembered combatants during the Forth Raid, but his was undoubtedly a great courage.

After Ferguson and the rest of Green Section had received their orders to patrol May Island, they proceeded with due haste to the designated spot. For a good ten minutes the three Spitfires circled the island waiting for further instructions. When the next order came, which was to stop orbiting and vector 360, the CO seemed to pay little heed. Douglas Farquhar maintained the monotonous orbit, seemingly oblivious to their new instructions. It was evident to Sandy Johnstone that the CO's R/T was cock-a-hoop. After realising the situation, Johnstone set about trying to attract Farquhar's attention. He eventually succeeded by waggling the wings of his Spitfire, at which the CO looked around to see him tapping his headphones. At once Farquhar seemed to grasp the situation, and realising that he had lost radio contact he signalled Sandy Johnstone to take over the section himself, immediately assuming station on Johnstone's port quarter.

Taking command of the section, Johnstone, accompanied by Ian Ferguson and Douglas Farquhar, steadily made their way north towards Dundee and the Firth of Tay. Intuitively, and encouraged by the controller's insistence that Bogeys lurked somewhere in the clouds, Green section scoured the heavens, praying to be the first into action. At 11.22a.m. an unidentified aircraft had been reported near Drem. This report seems to have been taken with a pinch of salt, as Green Section's instruction from Turnhouse was: 'investigate if you think necessary.' Green Section decided to continue northwards but their search remained fruitless. Nothing but sea, sky and cloud. Somehow Johnstone could still feel their presence. It was like looking for a needle in a haystack, but something told him they were out there. Something convinced him that against all the laws of probability, the enemy were coming, and coming towards Edinburgh; not the south.

Frustrated and low on fuel, Green Section was ordered back to base. Unfortunately, a strong southerly airstream had drifted them increasingly northwards, until they appeared to be about forty miles or so east of Peterhead across the North Sea.

The section had been airborne for at least an hour and their fuel was beginning to run critically low. At the most they had fifteen minutes grace. The CO, Douglas Farquhar, was still out of verbal contact with

Ferguson or Johnstone, who decided, rather than risk it back to Drem, they would make for the Coastal Command airstrip at Leuchars. Safely down, the ground crew at Leuchars who had precious little experience on Spitfires, as they mainly worked on Hudsons, set about the task of refuelling their unexpected guests. Douglas Farquhar took the opportunity to telephone Turnhouse in order to get permission for himself and his brother officers to adjourn to the Officers' Mess for a spot of lunch, while the groundcrew did their stuff. Permission was given, so that's exactly what they did.

Meanwhile back at Drem itself, Flight Lieutenant George Pinkerton took Blue Section up for another patrol at 11.39am. On this occasion Pinkerton, Archie McKeller and Paul Webb patrolled the skies above St Abb's Head, a piece of land sticking out into the North Sea just north of Eyemouth. Whether or not Blue Section had the same gut feeling as some of the other pilots I don't know. However, by the fact that one section or another was airborne almost continuously, it would seem that the Operations Room at Turnhouse was playing it safe. There have been a number of criticisms over the years, mostly aimed at the operations room or the Observer Corps, suggesting that the raid was detected late, or totally misread. Wherever the fault lay, it was pretty obvious that the Observer Corps was carrying out its duties to the letter, as there seems to have been, in my humble opinion, a great deal of air activity throughout the morning of 16 October; most of which would not have occurred if it had not been for the continuation of tracks coming in from the Observer Corps. The radar screen, remember, wasn't fully developed and it definitely had its problems that day. Nevertheless, again it was obvious that the radar screen was doing its job by the fact that raiders were detected approaching the coast. Fifty years later it's very hard to know where the fault occurred, but it's my sincere belief that the Observer Corps and the radar screen did all they could under the circumstances; and as I emphasise, the above-average level of air activity was proof of that fact.

Blue Section's patrol was consequently fruitless and Pinkerton landed his Spitfires back at Drem at 12.43p.m. without seeing anything.

At 12.25p.m. the Drone Hill radar station went out of service as the replacement amplifier valves were being fitted; at which time the formation of enemy bombers was well on its way to Scotland, heading almost directly towards it. Drone Hill may well have been an important radar establishment for its area, but its shut down was far from disastrous.

Hugh Barkla was in the Filter Room at RAF Fighter Command Headquarters at Stanmore in Middlesex, at the height of the flap. According to him, although the radar station at Drone Hill was out of action, Pohle's formation had been tracked continuously by the Chain Home radar stations on the east coast at Saxton Wold, Danby Beacon and Ottercops Moss. Barkla recalls that the junior officers and scientists at Stanmore were in no doubt that the formation was hostile. Barkla thought it was possible that, at this early stage in proceedings, unfiltered plots might have been fed direct to the sector airfield at Turnhouse. Indeed, an RAF report noted, 'The Post Office will not guarantee the ringing or speaking on our private line at Drone Hill because there is only one ringing set and handset for two lines (Stanmore and Turnhouse) which have to be paralleled.' As late as 1941, unfiltered plots were being passed direct to Turnhouse though these were considered unreliable.

On 16 October Hugh Barkla was at Stanmore attending an interview for the position as a Scientific Observer, when the raid suddenly began to materialise. He recalls: 'My future colleagues seemed pleased with the way that the radar chain had behaved. Drone Hill having been off the air for part of the day was not crucial. Even at that early date there was reasonable overlap of coverage on the East and South Coasts for aircraft at 10,000 feet or more, at least, and the raid had been under unbroken observation.'

The battle which took place on 16 October 1939, was of course, not merely a success story for the pilots of 602 and 603 Squadrons, nor the Auxiliary Air Force as a whole; it was also the baptism of the Spitfire. No matter what anybody says about the Spitfire, and how it was really the Hurricane that won the Battle of Britain, and all those traditional clichés we are continually blitzed by, the Spitfire remains the apotheosis of British Bulldogism, at the height of our nation's greatest peril.

Reginald Mitchell and the design staff of Supermarine Aviation, which was a subsidiary of Vickers Ltd, had begun to develop a high-speed single-seat fighter aircraft in the early 1930s, very much based on the experience they had gained when designing high-speed seaplanes for the Schneider Trophy Contests at the time. The Spitfire and Hawker's Hurricane were designed, manufactured and tested, almost at the same time. One stuck rigidly to the principles and doctrine developed and dictated by experience and experimentation. Nothing was left to chance, and ultimately, the Hurricane emerged to be one of the greatest aircraft designs we have ever seen, and without it history may well have turned for the worst. The Hurricane shot down more enemy aircraft during the Battle of Britain, than all the other types of aircraft put together. But the Spitfire, now that was something different. The Spitfire went beyond rigid formality, combining the technology needed to do the job, with artistic creativity, and the intuitive flair of a genius.

I ONLY CAME IN FOR THE DANCING!

The Spitfire also added another important weapon to our arsenal – the Germans were terrified of it. This fact is established later, when we interview the first German pilots who were shot down over Britain during the Second World War. Their greatest concern when they set out from their base at Westerland that day, was the prospect of running into Spitfires. In 1940, the Spitfire was the symbol of the nation's defiance, but German respect and fear of this little aircraft was evident, even before the Battle of Britain had started.

CHAPTER TWO

A GREAT AND VALIANT SQUADRON

The morning's activities had been controlled by the Operations Room at Turnhouse, which was in the centre of the airfield. This was a heavily-protected, self-contained, air-conditioned block; no windows, bomb-proof doors, and a rubble-filled roof many feet thick. It was manned by about forty people – plotters, controllers, and representatives of the Navy, AA guns, Observer Corps, searchlights, and all the runners. In the centre of the room was the plotting table, covered with a huge map on which WAAFs, like croupiers, were pushing counters to show the movements of planes. On the back wall was a map dotted with flickering lights, to show the fighter squadrons available. On a dais in front of this map sat the Controller, Squadron Leader Bob Johnstone, in direct contact with Newcastle HQ of No 13 Group, Fighter Command, and with his pilots by R/T when they were in the air. As Sector Controller, Bob Johnstone was thus able to build up a complete picture of the progress of any raid and would also be able to see the condition and availability of the fighter squadrons within his sector. He would know exactly their state of readiness and, if a squadron was in the air, he would also be immediately aware of its location. In this way he would be able to conduct the movements of all his available aircraft against the raiders. He would also have information concerning the weather and cloud conditions readily at hand.

On Bob Johnstone's left sat Flight Lieutenant Tommy (Tiger) Waitt, the senior operations B officer. In front of him was a telephone and switchboard, through which he was in direct contact with the squadron control officers of 603 and 602 Squadrons at Turnhouse and Drem respectively. As the Controller, eyes glued to the plotting map, gave out the orders, Tommy Waitt relayed them to the squadrons concerned and jotted them down on a piece of paper which the Controller initialled and passed on to the teleprinter for filing in Newcastle.

As the events of the day began to unfold, early warning and other relevant information was transmitted to No 13 Group Fighter Command Headquarters at Newcastle, where the Air Officer Commanding No 13 Group, Air Vice-Marshal Richard Saul, was later to become involved with the action himself through his direct telephone link with Bob Johnstone.

In October 1939 Britain was divided into four Fighter Command Groups. No 13 Group, commanded by Richard Saul, covered Scotland and the north of England; No 12 Group, commanded by Air Vice-Marshal Trafford Leigh-Mallory, covered the Midlands and most of Wales; No 10 Group, under the command of Air Vice-Marshal Sir Quintin Brand, was responsible for South Wales and the west of England; and finally, No 11 Group, under Air Vice-Marshal Keith Park – which was to bear a high percentage of German raids throughout the Battle of Britain – guarded the City of London and an area from the Isle of Wight to the east coast. Fighter Command Headquarters for the battle was at RAF Bentley Priory, Stanmore in Middlesex. It was from here that Air Chief Marshal Hugh Dowding, the Commander-in-Chief of Fighter Command and his staff, were able to build up a complete picture of the raid; which started on receipt of radar tracks from the Chain Home stations along the east coast.

The sector controller Bob Johnstone, would issue his orders based on his study of the operations room map. He would put enough aircraft into the air to intercept raiders, or to cover vulnerable points. He would not want to waste his resources by sending aircraft out unnecessarily, but at the same time it was his duty to keep a constant watch on those resources. He would have to know, for instance, whether aircraft were being refuelled or re-armed, and therefore vulnerable to attack. Using the comprehensive tracks available to him, Bob Johnstone's main task would be to direct the Spitfires of 602 and 603 Squadrons until they engaged the enemy. At this point, once a pilot had transmitted his 'tally-ho' message, the battle was left very much in the pilot's own hands. However, Johnstone would still be able to contact his pilots by radio telephone, and dictate their actions if he saw fit. This might happen if a new wave of raiders had appeared on his map and it looked as though they were heading for a vulnerable area. It is easily seen then, how important was the continued receipt of information from the Observer Corps and the radar screen was, even during the course of the battle.

I have very much stressed the importance of the Observer Corps, but how was it deployed, and how did it work on the day? As soon as an aircraft came into view and was identified as an enemy by an observer at an observation post, the observation post would report its height, direction, nationality and type to the Area Centre, via its direct telephone link. In turn, the Area Centre would pass the necessary information to the Fighter Command Sector Operations Room. Sector would then process this information to alert the various other parts of the air defence system – fighter stations, anti-aircraft gun positions, searchlight and balloon units, police and fire brigade. All the observation posts had been built in positions on high ground from where they could command an uninterrupted view for as far as possible. The most important job of a post was to identify the aircraft in the first place. So each Observer had to know not only how to recognise both enemy and friendly aircraft by sight, but also if possible by distinguishing different engine sounds. This was particularly useful at night, for observation had to be maintained around the clock. Whether or not the identification of aircraft by sound alone was reliable, however remains a matter of controversy. In fact, the Germans did not synchronise the engines of their multi-engined aircraft, as the British did, giving them a characteristic and distinctive engine note. Furthermore, the Luftwaffe's only four-engined bomber, the FW Kondor, was rarely employed over Britain. Hence identification by sound, to someone well-trained and experienced, might have been easier than at first appears.

Having observed and reported an enemy aircraft, the observation post would maintain its reports until it was well out of sight. By that time the Area Centre would already be receiving information about the aircraft from the next observation post on its flight path. The enemy plane would be plotted in this fashion until such time as it turned away or had been shot down by one of our defences.

From their lonely posts the Observers could provide a wide range of other useful services to the authorities, such as the reporting of fires, black-out offences, suspicious acts, or when and where bombs had been dropped. They could also report on the progress of aerial battles and, at times, give the location of a crashed aircraft. This last service was to prove very important on 16 October, as it is due to the Observer Corps (among other sources) that we know the exact time that the Ju 88 flown by *Hauptmann* Helmut Pohle had been brought down, and more importantly, whom was therefore the first successful pilot in shooting down a raider over Britain during the Second World War: was it Patsy Gifford of 603 Squadron, or George Pinkerton of 602 Squadron. Both of them must have felt sure it was him at the moment it happened – and for some time afterwards.

Throughout that morning, there had been a certain amount of bustle in the Ops room, as reports continued to come in of reconnaissance intruders in the area; first from the radar screen, and then from the various spotters. Tommy Waitt was due to go off duty at 1p.m., but he was asked to stay on.

At 1p.m., Flight Lieutenant George Pinkerton and Flying Officer Archie McKellar settled down to a quick lunch of Mulligatawny soup and ham sandwiches in the dispersal hut at Drem. They talked excitedly about their first encounter with an enemy aircraft. They wondered whether their bullets had hit the mark. Had they caused any damage? Nevertheless, the squadrons were unperturbed at the mornings events; there had been little to suggest that anything serious was in the offing. During the preceeding weeks, German reconnaissance aircraft had often been observed over Scotland. Admittedly this was the first time that contact had been made with the enemy, but that was no reason to suspect that their intentions were any more sinister than on previous occasions. After five or six weeks of continual alertness, and patrols that found nothing, many of the pilots were becoming sceptical of their chances of ever seeing an enemy plane, let alone shooting one down.

602 Squadron's CO, Squadron Leader Douglas Farquhar flying with Green Section, was still at Leuchars airfield on the other side of the Forth, where he, Sandy Johnstone and Ian Ferguson had retired to the relative sanity of the Officers' Mess for lunch. After a fruitless morning of chasing shadows through an endless sky, even Sandy Johnstone was beginning to feel that perhaps his intuition was wrong; perhaps nothing was going to happen after all. In the Ops Room at Turnhouse there were few suspicious pointers that a major air raid was about to take place.

At this point, although pilots were sitting down to lunch, there were still a few who suspected that something was up. But where were they, and when were they coming?

Just as 602 Squadron waited anxiously at Drem, so did 603 at Turnhouse. Red Section was comprised of Flight Lieutenant Patsy Gifford, Flying Officer Ken Macdonald and Pilot Officer Colin (Robbie) Robertson. Gifford flying Spitfire L.1070 (XT A) was destined to be a major player in the game which followed.

603 (City of Edinburgh) Squadron was formed at Turnhouse on 14 October 1925, and remained there up until the outbreak of the Second World War; fourteen years later. Their first aircraft, the DH 9A arrived in October 1925. They were later equipped with Wapiti in March 1930; Hart in February 1934; Hind in February 1938; Gladiator II in March 1939; and Spitfire I in September 1939. The Gloster Gladiator was the last biplane fighter of the RAF, entering service in February 1937. It was an extremely manoeuvrable aircraft with four Browning machine-guns.

The Squadron had been formed by Squadron Leader James A.

M'Kelvie, AFC, who had been a Major in the Royal Flying Corps during the First World War. When they received their very first DH 9A, as well as two Avro 504Ks for training purposes, he watched them bank towards the Pentland Hills. He pointed his shooting stick at a flock of peewits who were flying out to sea in perfect formation and said, "Some day 603 will fly like that. Or better still," he went on "hunt like that fellow over there." A hawk was passing in swift flight over the stubble.

Wisely guided and controlled by a succession of able commanding officers – Squadron-Leaders M'Kelvie, Murray-Philipson, Lord Nigel Douglas-Hamilton, and E. H. Stevens – 603 came to be regarded as one of the most efficient squadrons of the Auxiliary Air Force. It was specially chosen to operate alongside regular units of the RAF in the biggest air exercises held in Great Britain. It created a record for flying untouched by any other Auxiliary squadron. When Empire Air Days displaced the annual Hendon Pageant the public were provided with a close-up view of the service at work at their own aerodromes. On Empire Day 1939, the public's interest was reflected by the visiting of an estimated one million people. Edinburgh's 1939 Empire Day was visited by Air Chief Marshal Hugh Dowding, who presented the squadron with the Esher Trophy, won for the best all-round efficiency among the Auxiliary units.

By 1939 Turnhouse had become synonymous with the Edinburgh Auxiliaries, although for a short period between August 1936 and March 1938, 603 Squadron shared their home with the regulars of 83 Squadron. The 'Harts' of Edinburgh no doubt looked on with envy at the super-charged 'Hinds' of 83.

Turnhouse had been opened as a training centre in the spring of 1916. The aerodrome was used by the Royal Flying Corps to prepare pilots for the war in France. There were two Flights, one of Shorthorns and one of Longhorns, which were housed initially in canvas hangars. Instructors and pupils lived in bell-tents and messed in a marquee. Officers under instruction flew only on the calmest of weather. W.D. Patrick KC, wrote in a pre-war 603 Squadron newsletter:

'At Turnhouse in my time there were more pupils than the instructors could keep employed, and I managed to get a good deal of shooting and amusement. We were extraordinarily ignorant, judged my modern standards, of all but the elements of the art of flying, and did the strangest things with our antiquated machines, because we knew no better. There was continually some strange incident happening; one pupil, who was trying his first solo landing, flew right in a hangar-door, crashed three machines, and escaped without a scratch; another thought he would like to show his nice new toy to some of his pals at the depot of his old regiment. He tried to land on the barrack-square at Redford, crashed his machine to ribbons, telephoned for a breakdown gang and walked into Mess.'

By October 1916 Turnhouse had greatly changed. One permanent hangar had been completed and others were under construction. Permanent living quarters were constructed in a nearby field, and the burn which bordered the aerodrome on the west, was covered in order to extend the airfield.

Some time in the winter of 1916-17 there was added to the establishment at Turnhouse a Flight of B.E.2 Es for defence against Zeppelins. W.D. Patrick recalled:

'Before they came we had a farcical evening over a Zeppelin scare. It was in October 1916, and some of us were dining in Edinburgh. An Officer from the Scottish Command came in and told us that warning had come through that a Zeppelin had passed over Newcastle flying towards Edinburgh. All instructors were ordered to report to Turnhouse at once to take up machines and attack. I have never discovered what genius at the Scottish Command issued that order. Our machines were Farman Shorthorns whose ceiling was about 5,000 feet and they could take an hour to get to that height. The Zeppelin, if any, were not likely to cross Edinburgh at less than 10,000 feet. We suppose we were intended to bridge the difference between 5,000 feet and the Zeppelin's 10,000 feet with rifle fire, for we had no machine-guns. In addition we had neither flares nor searchlights to land by, and it was a certainty that we should crash every machine we took up. Fortunately the Squadron Commander got in touch with the Wing Commander by telephone to Newcastle and by the time we got to Turnhouse the order was washed out.'

By the end of the First World War Turnhouse had been transformed completely, with excellent hangars, workshops, and quarters, which in 1925 made a wonderful inheritance for Squadron Leader M'Kelvie and the Auxiliaries of 603 Squadron.

1936 was a particularly important year, due to the arrival of 83 Squadron. 603's CO, Squadron Leader Lord Nigel Douglas-Hamilton wrote in a letter to the squadron, dated 25 December 1936:

'This year clearly marks the dividing line between the old and the new Turnhouse. War-time buildings are being gradually swept away or reconstructed beyond recognition, and are giving place to buildings which are not only warmer, but in every way better adapted for their purposes.

'During the year no fewer than eight distinct sections have been rehoused, and the greater convenience of these new buildings will, it is hoped, be reflected in the quality of work done. It is interesting to notice that the length and usefulness of these old buildings must have far exceeded anything that could have been anticipated by those who planned them.

'There is another change that is even more important. Just ten years after the genesis of 603 Squadron, 83 Squadron entered upon the difficult and trying process of formation. I am glad to welcome its personnel and that of Station Headquarters to Turnhouse in the hope that their stay will be profitable, and that the memory of these early months will not be altogether an unpleasant one.'

The AOC, Air Commodore J. C. Quinnell DFC wrote at the time: 'Turnhouse now accommodates a Regular as well as an Auxiliary Air Force Squadron, and the Officer Commanding No 603 Squadron has the unique distinction of being the first Auxiliary officer to command a Station on which Regular as well as Auxiliary units are under his command.'

The co-habitation with 83 Squadron lasted until March 1938, when the regulars were moved to Scampton, which left the Edinburgh Auxiliaries sole occupiers at Turnhouse once again.

603 Squadron took over the administration of Turnhouse on 15 April 1938, following the closure of Station Headquarters. The Adjutant, Flight Lieutenant F. Tyson (a regular officer) made the following report in December 1938.

'On 1 July the new conditions of service in the Auxiliary Air Force came into force, involving a big change in the accounting procedure. On 27 October the squadron ceased to function as a bomber squadron, and was transferred from No 6 (Auxiliary) Group in the Bomber Command to No 13 Group in the Fighter Command. This again necessitated enormous internal reorganisation, the extent of which has not been fully realised by most of the airmen. It is entirely due to the industry of the officers and NCOs in charge of the Flights and Sections and the readiness with which they have undertaken the extra work involved, that these changes have taken place so smoothly.

'Especial mention must be made of those airmen and civilian clerks who for many weeks now have worked overtime amounting, in some cases, to as much as their normal working hours.

'The past year has been an unforgettable experience for us all, and I

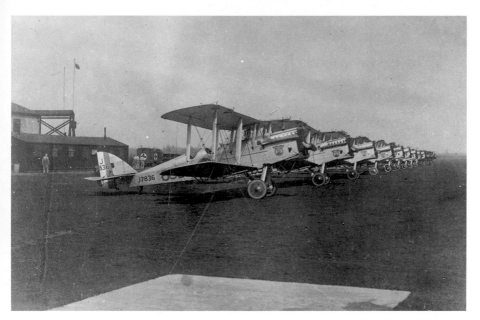

When 602 and 603 Squadrons were formed in 1925, their first aircraft, along with many other Auxiliary units, were Airco DH 9As. This photograph shows DH 9As of 605 (County of Warwick) Squadron. *(Photograph courtesy of Sir Hugh Dundas)*

A Spitfire of 602 Squadron on patrol over the Firth of Forth. Below is one of the old V&W Class Destroyers dating from the First World War, almost certainly HMS *Valorous*, used to escort east coast convoys.
(Photograph courtesy of Andrew Jeffrey/602 Squadron Archives)

An old photograph of the Forth Rail Bridge, prior to the building of the Forth Road Bridge. This is exactly how both German and British pilots would have seen the bridge in October 1939. Inch Garvie Island can be clearly seen.

(Photograph courtesy of George Mullay)

A famous photograph of some of the pilots of 602 Squadron in front of the Watch Office at Drem. *Left to Right:* Flying Officer Finlay Boyd, Flight Lieutenant George Pinkerton, Flight Lieutenant Sandy Johnstone, Flying Officer Paul Webb, Flying Officer A. M. Grant and Flying Officer Nigel Graeme. *(Photograph courtesy of Sir Hugh Dundas)*

Pilots of 603 Squadron pose proudly in front of Spitfire L1070 XT-A. *Left to Right:* Flying Officer Jim 'Black' Morton, Flying Officer John Young, Flying Officer Ian Ritchie, Flight Lieutenant Patsy Gifford and Flying Officer Colin (Robbie) Robertson. *(Photograph courtesy of Andrew Jeffrey)*

Group Captain Sir Hugh Dundas CBE, DSO, DFC, DL.
(Photograph courtesy of The Yorkshire Post*)*

Patrick 'Patsy' Gifford of 603 (City of Edinburgh) Squadron, who was the first pilot to shoot down a German aircraft over Britain during the Second World War. The Ju 88 flown by *Oberleutnant* Sigmund Storp crashed into the Forth off Port Seton at 2.45pm on 16 October 1939. *(Photograph courtesy of Sir Hugh Dundas)*

George Pinkerton of 602 (City of Glasgow) Squadron, who was largely responsible for shooting down the Ju 88 flown by *Hauptmann* Helmut Pohle into the sea near Crail at 2.55pm. 602 had lost out to 603 as the first squadron to draw blood by a mere ten minutes.
(Photograph courtesy of Sir Hugh Dundas)

Archie McKellar of 602 (City of Glasgow) Squadron, who played an important part in bringing down Helmut Pohle's aircraft on 16 October 1939, and who was responsible for the first enemy aircraft shot down on the British mainland during the Second World War, twelve days later.
(Photograph courtesy of Sir Hugh Dundas)

must thank all the personnel concerned for so loyally giving their support.

'There is much more to be done; more changes still to be made, but changes which will relieve us of much of the administration of the station and so enable us to concentrate on an aim for which we must all work – making this squadron, in its new role as a fighter squadron, worthy of its place in the Air Defence of this country.'

At the time of being mobilised 603 Squadron consisted of 23 officers, 19 NCOs and 97 other ranks; there was also one pupil pilot in the shape of R. Mackay who was a local travel agent. The Commanding Officer, Squadron Leader E.H. Stevens, was a writer for the *signet* in his civilian occupation.

Flight Lieutenant Patrick (Patsy) Gifford was one of the pilots of 603 Squadron who seemed to live a Jekyll and Hyde sort of existence. During the week, he was a respectable and respected solicitor in Castle Douglas (Kirkcudbrightshire); he was the burgh procurator fiscal and a town councillor. He was twenty-nine when he was mobilised in 1939 with the rest of 603, and had been a squadron member since 1931. But for many years, ever since he had studied law in Edinburgh during the early thirties, Gifford had thrown off the legal trappings every weekend. The furled umbrella was left behind beside the roll-top desk, and Gifford would race to Edinburgh in his fast Frazer-Nash for two glorious days of carefree flying (and often two evenings in midweek, too). He was immensely interested in aviation, and immensely proud of his car. His boast that he could do 'ninety in third' became a sort of squadron war-cry, and he used to claim that he could do the 95-mile journey from Castle-Douglas to Edinburgh in 80 minutes. The local police knew his car well, and though they often laid traps for him, they never managed to catch him. He was a great weekender, with all the public school sporting attributes necessary for success. In addition to being handsome, he was a fine shot, and excelled at tennis, cricket, rugby, and skiing. He was awarded a DFC and promoted to squadron leader for his part in shooting down Sigmund Storp's plane into the sea off Port Seton. The citation also mentioned his part, a week later, in bringing down another plane off St Abb's Head, when it was interfering with a convoy. A few days later, he helped to down a plane on to a hill near Haddington. This was the Heinkel He 111 accredited to Archie McKeller of 602 Squadron; the first enemy aircraft brought down on the British mainland. He was transferred to lead No 3 Hurricane Squadron, in France, and was killed in the spring of 1940.

On 16 October 1939, 603 Squadron was destined to shoot down its first enemy aircraft. Some time later, when stationed at Hornchurch with 100 Huns in the bag, Group Captain 'Daddy' Bouchier, the station commander said:

> 'No squadron was ever regarded more highly. No squadron ever went to war with such quiet grace, with so little fuss or with more determination.
>
> 'During the whole time they were with me – and they did not leave until the Battle of Britain was over and won – I never heard them complain once.
>
> 'Number 603 Squadron were not a squadron of giants. They were not even a squadron of personalities. I'm sure they will not mind me saying that.
>
> 'Number 603 Squadron were composed of a collection of quiet and serious young men. Men from the city desks of Edinburgh and the fields of the Lothians . . . a great and valiant squadron.'

Yellow Section of this great and valiant squadron on 16 October 1939, consisted of Flight Lieutenant George Denholm, Pilot Officer 'Sheep' Gilroy and Pilot Officer Jim 'Black' Morton. Each one of them, undoubtedly a personality of sorts. Pilot Officer Gilroy's unusual nickname, 'Sheep', was awarded to him due to the fact that before the war he had been a Lothian sheep farmer. In the years ahead, Gilroy was to become CO of 603 Squadron himself between 1946 and 1949.

George Denholm who had been a timber merchant in Bo'ness, also went on to command 603 Squadron and earn the affectionate nickname 'Uncle' George. Some people dubbed him 'Demon' after his exploits in 1940. He recollects those early days:

> 'We did no training as far as I remember in the first days of the war but waited continually for things to happen. We had however followed the prescribed Fighter Command training, but in practice they were not carried out according to the "book". The airfield at Turnhouse was grass and it happens I myself got ignominiously bogged in the middle of the Forth raid.
>
> 'Gifford absolutely loved flying and he utterly relished the war when it came. He did not drink, because he did not like it, but would sometimes have a glass of sherry to show he was prepared to join in occasionally. I think his mother was American and was very charming, a quality which he inherited to a fair degree. In the phrase of the time he could shoot an imperial line – for example about being upside-down (airborne) "With nothing on the clock". Another side of his character was that he gave a lot of thought to the technicalities of air-fighting and I think he was the first man I ever heard decry the bullet pattern used for eight-gun fighters at the beginning of the war. He soon decided it was useless. He left us to command No 3

Squadron and I believe he was killed after chasing a Hun too far into his own territory.'

At 1.26p.m., Red Section of 602 Squadron was ordered up to patrol Crail at Angels Five. Something was in the wind. At 2.19p.m., Blue Section of 602 at Drem was ordered to stand-by. Pinkerton ran to his Spitfire, L.1901, with the two other pilots of his section, Archie McKellar and Paul Webb. The engines were warmed-up.

At 2.22p.m., Flight Lieutenant Cairns Smith in the Drem Watch Hut relayed the message that Blue Section was to patrol Dalkeith at Angels Twenty. Blue Section took off, and the other readiness pilots settled down to a game of ludo (at 1/- a corner) in the flight hut. Ludo was all the rage at that time, because it could so easily be interrupted and re-started again.

In the dentist's room at Drem, the newly-married Flying Officer Finlay Boyd, settled himself apprehensively into the dentist's chair and obediently opened his mouth.

Robert Finlay Boyd was later to become another of the great auxiliary pilots with 602 Squadron. He brought down two Ju 87s and three Bf 109s in August 1940. In September of the same year he got three Me 109s and a Do 17. His score had gone up to twelve by the end of the Battle of Britain, and twenty by the end of the war: he was also to receive the DFC and DSO. Unquestionably, one of his luckiest encounters with the enemy happened in August 1940 while the squadron was based at Westhampnett near Portsmouth. On the day in question the order to scramble was received so late, that by the time the pilots – who had been in the mess having lunch – reached their aircraft, Stukas were already diving down at the airfield. Finlay Boyd had barely taken off when a Stuka dived right in front of him. He hadn't even had time to pull his wheels up, when instinctively he turned his firing button and blew the aircraft into the ground. The Stuka exploded! Finlay Boyd was so shaken by the experience that after he had completed a circuit of Westhampnett, he landed his Spitfire and sat out the rest of the mêlée. In later months Finlay Boyd was to prove his worth time and time again, fearless against the enemy. However, on 16 October 1939 his immediate fear was of a different strain, the enemy of different colours, namely the dentist!

At Turnhouse, the readiness pilots of 603 (City of Edinburgh) Squadron hung about the dispersal huts. There was no alarm yet and Flying Officer Ian Ritchie and two other pilots had been given the afternoon off, and were arriving in Edinburgh by car. Alastair Grant of 602 Squadron mentions the raid in his diary entry for the day, but told me:

'I missed out, being on short leave and visiting my girl friend in Edinburgh. I was considered a "late entry" at 602 as I travelled to Glasgow from Inverness each weekend, and was generally too tired and old to take much interest in killing Nazis!'

603 Squadron's Mess Secretary was also the unit's padre, Squadron Leader the Reverend J. Rossie Brown. After lunch he was preparing to visit Pilot Officer Hunter who was in the Military Hospital at Edinburgh Castle; little suspecting that his trip in the station car would be rudely interrupted, before it even began.

Squadron Leader J. Rossie Brown MA, was one of the great pre-war characters of 603 Squadron, who often dined out with the substantially true story of an AAF padre.

His story told of a pre-war visit to Jerusalem, when he awakened the Station Adjutant at Command Headquarters. Before the Adjutant stood – what appeared to be – an Air Force Chaplain, with the substantive rank of Squadron Leader denominated upon his sleeve. On the padre's lapel was an unfamiliar and baffling letter 'A'. 'What did A stand for?,' the Adjutant enquired?

You will note from this that Squadron Leader Rossie Brown sported only one letter 'A'. He should have worn two, one on each lapel. Unfortunately, the second 'A' had been pinched on the previous evening in the purlieus of King David Street, by a beautiful Arabian houri, who wanted it as a keepsake of his manly and attractive bearing – so the story went.

Rossie Brown explained to the Adjutant that he was an Auxiliary Air Force padre.

'An Auxiliary Air Force Padre!' growled the Adjutant incredulously. 'Never heard of such a thing.'

The story eventually led to the Adjutant arranging for the padre to fly to Baghdad in Iraq. Leaving Jerusalem by the Jaffa Gate, through which Lord Allenby had entered the Holy City when it surrendered to the British Army in 1917, the padre was driven the seven miles to Kolundia. These seven miles which took him past Nebi Samwil, where Samuel was buried; Ain Karim, the home of Zacharias and Elizabeth, and birthplace of John the Baptist; and Kubeibeh, the ancient Emmaus, where Christ broke bread with two of His disciples after His Resurrection and before His Ascension. Soon the padre was flying across the River Jordan.

Some time, and many adventures later, The Reverend Rossie Brown extracted himself from the Wapiti at Rutbah, where he looked forward to breakfast. However, the RAF of Iraq Command were keen to continue the journey, and had provided a flight of three Wapitis; one to transport the padre, and two for luggage and to act as escort.

Still babbling of his breakfast, the padre was encased again within a Wapiti. Accustomed as he was to Harts, this was a hardship, but he bore it, despite his crying want of food.

To cut a long story short, the three aircraft became enveloped in a whirling sandstorm and consequently separated. The pilot endeavoured to effect a landing. Since the ground was invisible at anything more than 150 feet, and since such ground as they did see was rocky and inhospitable, it was a hazardous undertaking. They continued on in the whirling opaqueness of the sandstorm, with the occasional swoop towards the ground revealing horrid possibilities of disaster. It was a nightmare flight that went on for three-quarters of an hour. Eventually, the pilot managed to get down, but admitted: 'I haven't the least idea of where we are, but thank God we're down.'

'Amen' said the padre.

'We may be here for days,' said the pilot pessimistically.

They were then surprised by the distant sound of singing voices and the drone of a motor vehicle. The padre blew the whistle he always carried and the pilot fired his Very pistol. But the miserable carload of humanity proceeded heartlessly on its way.

Darkness was not very far off, but before making final arrangements for the night, the pilot and the padre made an expedition in the direction of the sounds they had just heard. Tearing their handkerchiefs into strips they attached pieces here and there to the scrub they passed, securing their safe return to the Wapiti. Tracks of a car were found at last, but no sign of it or its 'musical' inhabitants. They retraced their steps, disappointed and disconsolate.

They fixed canvas coverings all over the more vulnerable parts of the aeroplane, and divided the night into watches. Eventually, the padre fell asleep.

When he awoke it was cold beyond his former experience – even by Turnhouse standards – and the wind got up in unbelievable velocity. In gusty torrents it assailed the travellers with undissembled fury, and threatened to capsize the Wapiti, anchored to the ground as it was.

The rest of the night the couple held onto the wings of the aircraft, lifted occasionally off their feet by the violence of the gale, but holding on for dear life all the same.

Sunrise was at 4a.m. The wind subsided and the atmosphere was clear. Eventually the pilot restarted the Wapiti and before long they were flying along the Euphrates, in glorious sunshine. They eventually reached Hinaidi, where at last, the Reverend Rossie Brown was able to enjoy a much appreciated and deserved breakfast – although a day late.

In these first two chapters I have outlined briefly the two squadrons which were about to do battle against the Nazi war machine, for the first time over Great Britain. It is important to understand the character of these two squadrons, and the men who were about to intercept the raiders. Remember at all times, these were not regulars: they were 'Weekend Flyers.' These were the same men who before the war, had worked and lived in Glasgow, Edinburgh and the Lothians. This point is particularly important to understand, because they were about to defend the same countryside that they had grown up in, and in which many of them, had lived and worked in all their lives.

CHAPTER THREE

TARGET ROSYTH

When *Oberleutnant* Gunther Prien in command of the German submarine U-47 slipped out of Keil on the early evening of 11 October 1939 and into the Kattegat the war was only six weeks' old.

On coming to periscope depth and sighting the lights of the Swedish port of Gothenburg U-47 turned west into the Skagerrak and set course on a journey of over 550 miles across the North Sea with the sole intention of sinking the 35,000-ton Royal Navy battleship, *Royal Oak*, then anchored in Scapa Flow, the fleet anchorage flanked by the Orkney Islands of Mainland, Burray, South Ronaldsay, Flotta and Hoy.

Scapa Flow had long been established as a safe haven and came to prominence during the 1914–18 war as a base for the Grand Fleet. In those days the only real threat to naval vessels at Scapa Flow would come as the result of a sea-borne attack either by enemy surface craft or less likely, submarines.

To counteract this unlikely eventuality the various accessible channels into the anchorage were heavily fortified with naval land-based guns and steps had been taken to partly block off some of the little-used passages.

Memories of the capabilities of the German Navy during the First World War were never far from the thoughts of the Lords of the Admiralty and in late 1937 it became apparent that once again Scapa Flow would attain a real strategic importance.

With Germany in the course of re-arming this was seen as the most likely threat. Portsmouth, Devonport and other bases in the South of England would be well within the range of aircraft operating from aerodromes on the west coast of Germany. Although this would result in having to avoid flying over Holland, Belgium and France.

There doesn't appear at that time to have been a great deal of thought given to the possibility that perhaps these countries might be subjugated, thus providing the Luftwaffe with bases sufficiently close to the

British mainland as to enable German bombers to reach most targets with relative ease.

Certainly Norway didn't figure in the equation and so it was that the Admiralty confirmed the continuing and uprated use of Scapa Flow as a naval base. Logically the location was ideal giving ready access to the northern areas of the North Sea and North Atlantic. Should hostilities break out with Germany, a Royal Naval force based in the Orkney Islands could effectively blockade any movement of German surface vessels attempting to set sail from Bremerhaven, Hamburg, Wilhelmshaven and Keil, as had been done twenty years earlier.

It was mistakenly thought that the extreme north of Scotland would be beyond the range of any German aircraft, such as the Heinkel He 111 and Junkers Ju 88, which were only twin-engined.

The age of the Dornier and the Focke-Wulf four-engined Kondor was still to come.

Scapa Flow was termed as a Fleet Anchorage – nothing more.

Rosyth on the north shore of the Firth of Forth, just to the west of the Forth railway bridge was however, a fully constituted Naval Base with dry dock and full refitting facilities.

As with Scapa Flow, Rosyth was ideally situated and could easily be defended from any type of attack carried out by enemy surface vessels.

Port Edgar naval base on the south bank of the Forth, opposite Rosyth was also the home of miscellaneous Royal Navy surface vessels including mine-sweepers.

While not quite so far from enemy aerodromes as Scapa it was nevertheless felt that to reach the dockyard area would involve a flight of over 450 miles of open sea, followed by a further 50 to 60 miles over mainland Britain, depending upon landfall.

With these false assumptions the Lords of the Admiralty slept soundly knowing that Portsmouth and Devonport were the most likely problem areas and that if the worst came to the worst, the pride of the Royal Navy would simply set sail and move lock stock and barrel northwards.

This sleep was rudely shattered during the early hours of Saturday 14 October 1939, two days before the Forth raid.

Late on the afternoon of the day before, U-47 came to periscope depth and Gunther Prien was to have his second view of the eastern approaches to Scapa Flow in just over a year.

During the summer of 1938 Prien had spent a short holiday in the Orkney Islands. He epitomised the character of an ordinary tourist, but he was in fact a submarine commander on leave and a fanatical Nazi into the bargain.

Armed with the ubiquitous sketch pad and a seaman's eye for detail he spent many hours in the vicinity of St Mary's and nearby Kirk Sound, illustrating accurately the approaches to Scapa Flow including some of the less likely approaches.

These sketches were to prove invaluable to the German High Command.

He was primarily interested in Kirk Sound where he observed that there were signs of impending defence works including the blocking of this route into the main anchorage.

Admiral Dönitz was quick to grasp the importance of Scapa Flow so far as the Royal Navy was concerned and was under no illusions as to the devastating effect capital ships of the Royal Navy could inflict upon German Shipping in the North Sea.

At that time priority was being given to the U-boat arm of the German naval forces and he was convinced that a pre-emptive strike against the Royal Navy was essential.

And so under cover of darkness, shortly after 5.00p.m. on the evening of Friday 13 October, U-47 on the surface, slipped silently and unseen through a narrow 50-ft gap in Kirk Sound and submerged to the bed of Scapa Flow.

Conscious that if his presence had been detected there would be no escape for him or his crew should it be necessary to withdraw under attack, U-47 maintained an absolute silence.

For seven hours the submarine lay on the seabed and just after midnight Prien brought the U-47 to periscope depth.

He wrote in his log that it seemed to be amazingly light and other reports of this particular action speak of there being an unusually prominent display of Northern lights – aurora borealis – a fairly common occurrence in these northern latitudes.

He quickly identified two large battleships and several destroyers.

At 1.00a.m. on the morning of Saturday 14 October, a salvo of torpedoes struck the *Royal Oak* and within ten minutes it had rolled over and sunk with horrendous loss of life.

In the confusion which followed Prien made no rash moves to escape in a hurry as he carefully picked his way past the obstructions meant to protect Kirk Sound.

By two in the morning he had reached the open sea and set course for Keil.

The reader might be forgiven for asking the question – what has this to do with the Forth Raid?

The truth is that it was not only Priens' sketches which enabled the successful penetration of the Scapa Flow defences. Much more accurate information was achieved by the Luftwaffe flying regular high-level photographic reconnaissance flights over Scapa Flow from their Westerland base on the island of Sylt.

Analysis of the series of photographs, taken from a Heinkel He 111 flying at 25,000 feet, revealed that in Kirk Sound a small steamer which had been deliberately sunk as a block ship had in fact been moved by the extremely strong tidal races through the narrows and had effectively provided a gap wide enough to allow the passage of a submarine on the surface. This was something which amateur artist Gunther Prien could not have been aware of one year earlier.

This attack immediately brought about some rather uncharacteristic and panic-stricken measures on the part of the Admiralty.

Units of the Home fleet, including several battleships and heavy cruisers, put to sea the following day with no clear cut plan of what to do next.

Rosyth was the obvious choice, as was the Firth of Clyde on the west coast of Scotland.

Given the will and the virtual freedom to exploit the situation, reconnaissance units of the Luftwaffe flying from the North Frisian islands off the coast of Germany shadowed the naval movements as best they could during daylight hours.

The bombing raid on the Firth of Forth was now only 48 hours away.

During the last few days of September and the first week in October units of the Luftwaffe flew regular photographic sorties using Heinkel He 111 twin-engine bombers.

Flying at a maximum altitude over the approaches to the Firth of Forth, Edinburgh and Rosyth Dockyard, the results, even by today's standards, were quite remarkable.

In the knowledge that they had already disposed of the *Royal Oak,* they were desperate to establish the whereabouts of other Royal Navy capital ships. Of particular interest to the German High Command was the location of the battleships, *Hood, Repulse, Rodney* and *Nelson,* together with the aircraft carriers *Ark Royal* and *Illustrious.*

While very occasionally there were attempts to intercept these flights, no physical contact was made.

Pre-flight planning ensured that the route taken across the North Sea would bring about a landfall somewhere between Dundee and Arbroath flying west towards Perth and Stirling and then turning east down the river Forth towards Rosyth, the Forth Bridge and Leith Docks.

At altitudes in excess of 20,000 feet, and flying at over 270 mph, the Germans thought the likelihood of the RAF being able to intercept these aircraft without prior knowledge, was almost non-existent. The Luftwaffe never fully appreciated the value of the British detection and reporting system, to Fighter Command. They underestimated the ability of our radar network, and no doubt looked upon the Observer Corps as a group of ageing boy scouts who liked to play at war – there were those in Britain who felt the same way.

This northerly route also avoided detection by the early warning systems at St Abb's Head on the Berwickshire coast which the Luftwaffe had photographed on several occasions at the beginning of October. However, Ian Brown, who is a considerable authority on the radar side of things, told me: 'I have a copy of the original German target documentation of Drone Hill and this makes it clear that the Germans were not aware in October 1939 that the site was a radar station.'

As early as 2 October, photographs had been taken over the Forth Bridge which showed the presence of several large warships at anchor.

The civilian population in and around the Edinburgh area had no idea that enemy aircraft regularly passed over their capital city in broad daylight, let alone the fact they were engaged in photography of such a high standard as to show motorcars queuing up to board the ferryboats at the Hawes Pier at South Queensferry, or tram-cars running along Lower Granton Road near the Port of Leith. The sirens were never sounded!

Magnification of the photographs clearly showed strategic targets in the Edinburgh area, including railway marshalling yards and stations, dock installations, electricity power stations and gas-works.

Had the man in the street been aware of these goings on and the fact that the aircraft used to take the photographs of their city and surrounding area were Heinkel He 111s – possibly even the same ones he had watched two years earlier on the cinema newsreels which showed the utter destruction of the Spanish town of Guernica by Germany's Kondor Legion, he might have been less inclined to stand and stare at the skies on Monday 16 October, only two days after the sinking of the *Royal Oak*.

Come that fateful day, not only the Royal Navy and the Royal Air Force, but also the entire population of Great Britain would come to realise that nowhere on the British mainland was beyond the reach of the Luftwaffe.

CHAPTER FOUR

HAND AND FOOT

On 16 October 1939 first lieutenant (*Oberleutnant*) – then aged twenty-five – Sigmund Storp looked to the skies. The sun shone; scarcely a cloud was to be seen. 'The right sortie weather,' he thought. He went to the phone at the airfield of Westerland on the island of Sylt, just off the coast of Denmark, and made a date with his girl friend, Elizabeth. He arranged to meet her at the weekend. He had no idea, when he put through the call, that he would not be seeing her for the next six years. He had no presentiment that 16 October 1939 would be a black day for him – with more than a few surprises. He little thought that on his second flight against England, he would be the very first pilot shot down by Spitfires.

The main topic at the base was how the battleship *Hood*, supposed to be in the Firth of Forth, could be dive-bombed. He had finished his phoning only a short time before the order came to set out. There seems to be great confusion about the actual number of German aeroplanes that were used in the raid that day. There is also confusion about their identity. Every article you read, or every book that gives mention to the subject, quotes different figures and types. In 1957 when Sir Hugh Dundas tracked him down, Sigmund Storp said the group consisted of twelve Ju 88s, under the command of *Hauptmann* Helmut Pohle. They were under orders to attack the *Hood*, at least. Many years later Helmut Pohle confirmed these figures himself.

For the bomber crews of 1 KG Verband who opted to live on the base at Westerland, it had already been a long morning. They were awakened a little earlier than usual, by the sound of Junkers Jumo twelve-cylinder engines, as two Heinkel He 111 aircraft of KG 26 gathered speed and bounced across the grass airfield. Heading west the two aircraft climbed rapidly in order to clear the banks of sea mist which were beginning to blow across the island of Sylt from the North Sea. The time was just 8a.m. and the results achieved by the crews of these two twin-engined reconnaissance aircraft were to have a direct bearing on the events which were to follow during the remainder of that autumn day.

Hauptmann Helmut Pohle watched until the two Heinkels were but distant specks in the western sky and silently wished them good luck, before making his way back to his flight office to prepare for his own departure, which was scheduled for 1.00p.m.

Helmut Pohle said of the morning in question:

'On 16 October 1939, HMS *Hood* was on her way to Rosyth in the early hours of the morning, and being shadowed by German maritime reconnaissance. I was based at Westerland as commander of the first *Gruppe* of *Kampfgeschwader* 30 (1 KG 30). At 8a.m. I got the order to attack the *Hood*, but only on sea. The order was quite definite. Do NOT attack when she is in dock. The powers in Germany at that time were still hoping there could be an agreement with England and civilian casualties should under no circumstances aggravate propaganda.'

Pohle hadn't slept all that well and had been preoccupied with the command logistics of ensuring the navigational integrity involved in guiding twelve fully-laden Junkers Ju 88s across 430 – 450 miles of open sea (depending on their eventual landfall) and then on to the specified target area a further 50 – 70 miles over the British mainland.

Previous reconnaissance flights over the area had not really been challenged to any great extent by the Royal Air Force, but these had involved single aircraft flying at high altitude. This would be the first time that so many aircraft would route together to the same target, and while he hoped for an element of surprise the navigational aspects kept niggling at his mind.

There is an equation called the one in sixty rule which holds good to this day. This states that an error of only one degree in a heading, will lead to an aircraft being one nautical mile off course after flying only sixty nautical miles. 1 KG 30 would be faced with a flight of some 370 nautical miles over open sea before any kind of visual fix could be expected. An error of one degree over this distance could lead to being six nautical miles off track. Now one degree out is of no great consequence when flying at 20,000 feet in good visibility, but with inaccurate weather actuals and variable wind speeds an error of five degrees becomes just a little more realistic and likely. The result of this would place the flight anything up to thirty nautical miles either north or south of the planned landfall.

The weather information, scant as it was, indicated a south-westerly air-flow over that part of the British mainland, but what speed, at what height? Suppose there was an in-flight miscalculation as little as five degrees, this could lead to twelve Ju 88s arriving in the mouth of the Firth of Forth off North Berwick, instead of Berwick-on-Tweed, and any element of surprise would have evaporated within minutes of flying over populated areas and would in effect route the bomber force on a westerly course directly over the aerodrome at Drem. Such a route would only compound the problem the further west they flew along the Firth of Forth.

With any fighter aircraft there might be at Drem alerted, Pohle knew his Ju 88s could be flying into a noose. Unfortunately for him, it appears that for once Luftwaffe intelligence was found wanting in this area, no-one could give him exact types, numbers and locations of British aircraft. With RAF Turnhouse ahead of him and Drem to the rear, anticipating their return, Pohle's concerns appeared on the face to be fully justified.

Pohle also accepted the need for the actual bombing runs to be made on a west to east heading, out of the sun, which also gave them a fast escape route with the wind behind them, whilst they climbed away, heading for the North Sea and safety. The old saying 'Beware the Hun in the sun', became a poignant reality later that afternoon.

He didn't relish the idea of having to carry out a shallow dive-attack on shipping less than a mile from the Forth Bridge into wind which would naturally lower his ground speed, presenting an easier target for AA guns, and afterwards, having carried out a relatively low-level attack be almost immediately faced with having to climb to avoid the bridge superstructure, where the tops of the cantilever spans were over 300 feet above sea-level.

Again, he confirmed to himself, it had to be west to east, and if he found himself flying up the Forth towards the target, so be it, but this would ultimately necessitate some flight deviation either to the north or south, to bring him into the correct flight path for his attack. This was Hobson's choice – to the north he would be faced with the RNAS at Donibristle and the anti-aircraft batteries which he knew protected Rosyth dockyard, whilst to the south would necessitate flying over Edinburgh and ultimately Turnhouse aerodrome, where intelligence sources had told him there was a squadron of Gladiator biplanes. As you will read later, not everything went according to this plan, and although most of the bombers did in fact manage their final approach on the target area from the south-west, others approached from different directions.

While Gladiator aircraft would not present Pohle and his aircraft with too many worries, there were unconfirmed reports circulating around his Westerland base that there might just be one or two Spitfires at Turnhouse. What might there be at Drem? Neither of these options particularly appealed to him and his thoughts gradually gave way to breakfast and the final briefing with his aircrews.

Talk in the Mess that morning among the crews would undoubtedly have revolved around rumours that one of their U-boats had penetrated the defences at Scapa Flow, in the Orkney Islands, north of Scotland, and had sunk a major battleship, and damaged several smaller ships which were at anchor.

Pohle reflected on the implications of this news, wondered if it was true, and concluded that the British would most certainly have intensified their vigilance, so far as the protection of their naval bases and vessels was concerned. This was good news indeed for Germany, but only added to Pohle's concerns for his mission; the success of which was entirely his responsibility.

Unknown to Pohle and the aircrews of 1 KG 30 as they left their morning briefing at about 10.00a.m., was the fact that one of the two Heinkel He 111s sent out to reconnoitre the target area, had been identified by the British Observer Corps and was at that very moment visual to the lookouts onboard HMS *Edinburgh*, anchored beside the Forth railway bridge. Some fifteen minutes later it would be sighted and engaged by Flight Lieutenant George Pinkerton and Flying Officer Archie McKellar of 602 Squadron in the vicinity of Dunbar, as it made good its escape out over the North Sea.

At 11.30a.m. both Heinkels were within wireless range of their home base. The transmission confirmed that conditions over the target area were good, with only a slight ground haze, a light south-westerly wind and broken cloud at 4,000 and 7,000 feet. Visibility was more than 30 miles.

The final piece of information relayed was by far the most significant. Spitfire aircraft had been seen operating in the area of Dunbar. Pohle immediately thought about Drem. A feeling of some apprehension penetrated his deepest thoughts, but nevertheless the raid, as planned, would proceed.

At 11.55a.m. twenty-four Junkers Jumo 211J engines shattered the silence surrounding Westerland as twelve aircraft taxied out from their dispersal points. By noon, with all take-off checks complete, the first group of three Ju 88s, each with a crew of four, lifted off from the grass field at Westerland, followed by the remaining nine in groups of three, at four-minute intervals.

The order was to dive-bomb HMS *Hood* and other fleet units at the Royal Naval Base at Rosyth, on the north side of the Firth of Forth, very near to the Forth railway bridge. But a Führer order made the task difficult. It saved, as was later apparent, the battleship *Hood* because that Führer order forbade the dropping of bombs on British soil.

Pohle's group assumed flight formation above Westerland – twelve bombers of the most up-to-date dive-bombing type, each with two high-explosive steel-encased bombs of 500 kilogram weight each. Experienced fighting-men manned the planes. Some of them had fought in Spain. They assembled at a height of 22,000 to 23,000 ft.

In Pohle's Junkers Ju 88 the first twenty minutes or so were spent checking and re-checking the performance of the aircraft; engine oil temperature and pressure, gyro compass with magnetic compass; wind speed and direction; ground speed and likely estimated time of arrival at the British coastline. This had been calculated as 2.00p.m.

As is common with all bomber aircrew there was some light hearted internal chatter, ranging from family matters to the likely duration of hostilities but after a while this died down. Provision for the crew of four was rather cramped in the front portion of the fuselage. The pilot was located on the left with the bomb-aimer opposite him but at a lower level. The upper rear gunner's position was immediately behind the pilot with the wireless operator placed behind the bomb-aimer, where he could also be called upon to operate the lower rear armament. All round visibility was excellent from the cockpit of the Ju 88, with a fully glazed fuselage nose. Both the pilot and rear gunner were positioned beneath a short section of transparent hood.

With a maximum speed of nearly 300 mph at 17,500 feet, the aircraft could climb to this sort of altitude in just twenty-three minutes. It had a service ceiling of 27,000 feet and could and indeed would be used as a shallow dive-bomber.

Sigmund Storp remembered the raid very well; after all it was destined to be his last.

'I shall never forget this raid as long as I live. Radio silence was ordered, to surprise the enemy, if possible. We crossed the North Sea at a speed of 400 kph an hour, in fine flying weather. Four men flew in each Ju 88 – the pilot, co-pilot, radio operator and gunner. All of us were tense in expectation. We knew it would be no Sunday afternoon stroll. The main question agitating all our minds, shall we get to our goal unnoticed. We held our English enemy in great respect, especially his Spitfires. For us it was still a gentlemen's war, and not yet the brutal affair it became later. Our machines flew steadily. We were busy keeping direction. Engines all going uniformly.'

Storp explained that during the monotony of the flight over the North Sea, he pondered his past experience as a pilot. The rest of his crew consisted of *Feldwebel* Hans Georg Hielscher, *Feldwebel* Hugo Rohnke and *Obergefreiter* Kramer.

Storp was a forester's son, born in 1914, and became interested in flying at a very early age. At seventeen he gained a diploma for fancy flying, and wanted to have a career as an officer. In 1932 he joined up – as a marine. As a cadet he sailed around the world, in the cruiser *Köln*, one of the highlights of which was a trip to Australia. The cadets, not yet travelling under the Nazi flag, knew how to win the hearts of the Australians. In Sydney and Melbourne thousands visited the ship daily to see the young Germans. After the world trip, Storp transferred to naval flying duties. He had an all-round training and tried out almost every type of plane available at that time. During the war in Spain he was in the Kondor Legion. What Korea was to the Americans and the British, the Spanish Civil War was for the Germans. As a marine pilot, Storp got to know how serious and hard war really was. He learned, with his comrades, how to take off and land at night, with a side wind rising over the river.

The Spanish war was decisive for the build-up and the tactical growth of the Luftwaffe. That was Storp's opinion in 1957. After nine months in Spain, Storp returned to the Luftwaffe testing base at Travemünde. The development of the Ju 87 (Stuka) and of the Ju 88 was hastened by the Spanish Civil War. At Travemünde Storp ranked as a veteran, in view of his experience in Spain. In August 1939 he was transferred to the air base at Rechlin, Mecklenburg, where in all calm the most modern flying group of the Luftwaffe consisting of Ju 88 dive-bombers was assembled. They were machines which had not been produced en masse, but came as a result of the first test products.

'It was at first unimaginable for us how it could be possible to turn these heavy birds weighing 17 tons downwards in a direct dive and then bring them up again. In the beginning it was no easy flying. In Rechlin we learned how to dive on pin-point targets.'

Ironically the Ju 88 was probably Germany's most suitable aircraft for bombing operations over Northern Britain. Its high diving speed and manoeuvrability meant that although it could not successfully engage British fighters in combat, it was certainly able to take evasive measures to ensure its survival. It might seem incredible, but an experienced Ju 88 pilot could give a Spitfire pilot a jolly good run for his money. It was also extremely rugged and could withstand quite a heavy pounding. No doubt the fact that the Luftwaffe only lost two aircraft that day, was partly due to a combination of these factors.

Evidently, due to their high level of battle experience in Spain and the intense training the pilots had undergone at Rechlin, the group of men who now headed towards Scotland would succeed if any one could. This was the intention from higher authorities at any rate. Storp goes on to explain how he first became involved with the conflict over the North Sea.

'When the war started I was transferred to Westerland with five Ju 88s. On 26 September 1939 I flew my first sortie towards England, with my formation (five machines). The order to fly came almost without notice. Two heavy English fleet units had been sighted in the North Sea. One was the carrier *Ark Royal.*

'We had orders to concentrate on the *Ark Royal.* There was bad weather, with rain squalls and hanging clouds and mist. In my formation I had a well-known German test pilot, Francke by name. He succeeded in hitting the *Ark Royal* with his bombs. I myself tried three times but could not hit, because of the bad visibility. The British ships fired all they had in their guns. After diving, I chased over the surface of the ocean, between the ships. Because I was just above the waves neither ship could fire on me: they would have hit one another. In the same part of the North Sea there was another British ship formation, resembling the one that we had attacked, in strength and number. We had reported our hits on the *Ark Royal,* and that we had seen smoke rising. A German recce plane which flew over this area a little later saw this second fleet formation and reported: "*Ark Royal* no longer to be seen." This error was responsible for the belief of higher authority that the *Ark Royal* had been sunk. We returned from this sortie without loss.'

'Where is the *Ark Royal?*' asked Lord Haw-Haw repeatedly during the last months of 1939. Aboard the carrier which the infamous broadcaster announced sunk, the ship's company rolled with laughter on the decks of the huge vessel, as they listened to his traitorous rantings. Poor *Oberleutnant* Francke, the pilot who scored the near miss and reported it, was decorated by Göring with the Iron Cross for sinking the *Ark Royal.* His brother officers, however, were not deceived by the unearned decoration he was forced to wear.

During the action which took place on 26 September, a Sea Skua of 803 Squadron, which was attached to the *Ark Royal* itself, and was piloted by Lieutenant B. S. McEwan, brought down a Dornier 18 flying boat. This was the first German aircraft to be shot down by British fire during the Second World War.

Hauptmann Helmut Pohle who led the raiders against the Firth of Forth was regarded as a first-class technical brain. He was a test pilot on Ju 88 and was able to go over the head of the Luftwaffe Chief of Staff direct to Göring and Hitler. Storp thought his orders for the Edinburgh raid came to Pohle direct – especially the order to bomb the *Hood* but not to drop bombs on British soil. Storp said the top men were specially chosen for this first mission, the best Ju 88 men, the idea being to guarantee success as far as possible to make a real hit with the idea that Britain would then be more likely to listen to Hitler and go along with him against Russia.

Pohle had arrived at Westerland on 9 October 1939 in command of the Luftwaffe's first *gruppe* of *Kampfgeschwader* 30 (1 KG 30). He was sent to the base to join KG 26 under the command of Karl Missy and LG I under Jocho Helbig. The idea behind his posting was to strengthen the North Sea Armada to approximately 150 bombers, all aimed at the destruction of the British home fleet and North Sea convoy system. Apparently, Helmut Pohle made his formidible presence felt from the moment of his arrival. It is recorded that he arrived on Sylt in a fury over the disastrous attempts the group had already made against the Royal Navy. No doubt the fiasco concerning Francke and the *Ark Royal* had also played a part in the Air Ministry's present state of embarrassment, for which Pohle was undoubtedly a spokesman. Indeed, It is known that prior to the raid on the Firth of Forth Helmut Pohle was ordered to attend a meeting in Berlin at the Air Ministry, presided over by Göring himself. The Luftwaffe chief of staff was recorded as saying: 'Pohle, we've got to score a success. Everyone who helps in getting rid of those ships will have a house of his own and all the medals that are going.' At the time Göring was getting frustrated by their inability to score a success, however small. He considered the Naval bases at Rosyth and Scapa Flow to be of paramount importance and he was anxious to step up the bombing against the British Fleet. One of the most incredible statements to be made at the Air Ministry meeting was made by the German Chief of Intelligence, Major Beppo Schmid. 'There's no fear of our bombers running into British fighters up there.' The Germans considered themselves to be the master race, to obtain an intelligence far superior to that of their state enemies. And yet the chief of their intelligence service, naïvely supposed that the British would not have protected an important Naval base with some kind of aerial insurance. This I find quite unbelievable, stupid even, but it is the absolute truth. And to emphasise the apparant lack of brain cells in the Luftwaffe hierarchy, Göring believed him implicitly. I very much doubt that Helmut Pohle would have been so naïve himself, but if he was, the knowledge he received on the morning of the raid, that Spitfires had been observed operating near the target area, would have been a severe shock to his system.

The Luftwaffe had gained a certain amount of aerial reconnaissance by sending aircraft over the Forth during the preceeding weeks. A German reconnaissance photograph published in New English Library's *History of Aviation* and dated 2 October 1939, clearly shows the radar station at St Abb's Head; although as Ian Brown confirmed earlier, the Germans didn't appreciate the relevance of the site. Similar photographs showed Leith docks and the area around the Forth Bridge, which go so far as to give details of anti-aircraft gun emplacements (*flakstellung*), and ship positions. Airfield locations around Edinburgh were certainly no secret, and reconnaissance aircraft had photographed both Drem and Turnhouse. Therefore Beppo Schmid must have been aware of the fact that several fighter squadrons were available in the area. He can be excused for writing off 602 Squadron, as they had only arrived at Drem on 13 October, three days before the raid. Thus, the photographs taken of Drem during the first week of October would not have shown evidence of their Spitfires anyway. But 603 Squadron had always been at Turnhouse, any intelligence source within Edinburgh itself could have told him that. 603 had received their Spitfires in September, so they would have been at Turnhouse during the reconnaissance period. However Helmut Pohle is quite adamant that: 'The attack order of the German General Staff said there were no Spitfires in Scotland.'

This particular air raid, and indeed a number which followed thereafter, went against the established Luftwaffe norm, when sending bombers deep into enemy territory. To enable the success of a raid without losing too many aircraft, the normal practice was to send a fighter escort, which could break off and engage the enemy as it tried to intercept the raid. This would mean that the Spitfires or Hurricanes would be busy in combat with the fighter escort, leaving the bombers unimpeded to carry out the business in hand. The raid on 16 October 1939 employed no fighter escort whatsoever, so Sigmund Storp, Helmut Pohle, and the other German pilots, knew very well that if they were attacked by British fighters, they would most likely be cut to pieces. The simple truth is that the fighter aircraft available to the Luftwaffe at the time, had too limited a range to make their use practical in raids against Scotland. Bomber pilots deployed against the east coast of Scotland, or 'Suicide Corner' as it became known for this very reason, took off from their European bases fully aware that they were completely on their own. Survival depended on their competence to fly the aircraft to the limits of its capabilities.

Helmut Pohle, the leader of the formation, was not a traditional strutting German officer type. He insisted on keeping a civilian haircut. He was normally quiet, and modest in speech. His outpourings on the day of his arrival at Sylt were the exception rather than the rule, but he had been placed in a responsible position. He was thought of very highly, and his appointment as the man who would give the Luftwaffe its first descisive victory was considered a high honour. He had worked on Ju 88s before they went into serial production, and knew them inside out.

Storp said of Pohle: 'He had a kind of sixth sense. He seldom spoke. When he did, what he said always had "hand and foot"'. (The German phrase 'hand and foot' means there was a good deal in what he said. Storp said in his view the aces, the top three, were used in the early days, the feeling in Berlin being that if the best efforts were put out first 'Britain could be forced to come to terms' – through the great successes of these aces. 'Until 16 October 1939 we spent our time in tactical exercises in the map room, studying the Firth of Forth. Small ship models were used as targets, and we made ourselves acquainted with the British ship silhouettes of different classes. We especially studied the *Hood*.'

Now came 16 October. At 12 noon *Hauptmann* Pohle took off from Westerland at the head of his 1 KG 30 Verband. Sigmund Storp said that for an hour-and-a-half he and his comrades spoke little, as they flew towards Britain.

The time was coming up to ten past one and already the first group of three Ju 88s were approaching the mid-point of their North Sea crossing.

Pohle's two Junkers Jumo engines were performing faultlessly and with the altimeter reading 23,000 ft, he instinctively started to scan ahead looking for tell-tale signs of the approaching coastline.

Well below him he was able to catch an occasional sighting of the sea between the clusters of cumulus clouds, and mentally noted that the wave crests appeared to confirm that the wind as reported by the reconnaissance Heinkels was indeed blowing from roughly the south-west.

This was something to remember for the return leg of the sortie. He tried some simple mathematical calculations in his head involving the use of reciprocal headings and quickly realised that if the wind speed happened to increase at all from the south-west he would need to be extremely careful about landfall on the Island of Sylt, otherwise he could find himself flying over the coast of Denmark, something which had to be avoided at all costs. Added to this he calculated that if all went according to plan it would be around five o'clock and almost dark when he came to make his final approach to Westerland.

Little did *Hauptmann* Helmut Pohle realise that his calculations would prove to be totally meaningless.

This was a perfect day for flying. Once again he scanned the horizon – but nothing. He was becoming impatient with the seeming lack of progress. The rhythmic pulse of the engines was almost soporific and had it not been for the cold he was certain he could easily have dozed off.

This was not good enough and his thoughts immediately turned to the battleship HMS *Hood*. Where would she be, what sort of fire power could it bring to bear on his group of aircraft, and just how alert would the defences be? Being in the first group might just give him the edge so far as the element of surprise was concerned – but he wasn't convinced. And what about the reports of Spitfires being active in the area. Pohle had never seen a Spitfire in the flesh but like countless members of his countrymen he had watched newsreels of the June 1937 Hendon air show where after various displays by Blenheim and Fairey Battle bombers a lone Supermarine Spitfire had suddenly burst upon the scene. Here indeed was a fighter aeroplane not to be trifled with. Fitted with a Rolls-Royce Merlin engine, this latest addition to the Royal Air Force was said to be capable of speeds in excess of 370 mph and was armed with eight .303 guns in the wings. Most disturbing to Pohle was the allegation that this single-seat interceptor had an initial rate of climb approaching 2,300 ft per minute. If 1 KG 30 was correctly identified as it overflew the British mainland, and if there were Spitfires in the area waiting, the consequences didn't bear thinking about. As far as the Germans were concerned, the Spitfire was Britain's secret weapon, they knew little about its destructive capabilitities, after all, it had never been used in combat before. The mystique, and mist of uncertainty which was building up around the Spitfire no doubt made their fear of it even worse.

Pohle's reflections were suddenly interrupted as his bomb-aimer enthusiastically told the crew that he could see the enemy coastline ahead, maybe twenty miles away. Pohle glanced at his watch. It was just on two o'clock and his group had about seventy miles remaining to get to the target area.

From now on it would be total concentration. British Ordnance Survey maps of southern Scotland bought openly in London a year earlier were carefully laid out between Pohle and his bomb-aimer.

The route was clearly marked starting from Berwick-on-Tweed, and the weather seemed to be improving the further west they flew.

Two small fishing trawlers appeared under the starboard wing and there was immediate discussion amongst the crew as to whether they might let the cat out of the bag. They didn't! But where were they and where had they crossed the coast?

To know the exact point at which the raiders crossed the coast, and their subsequent flight path, we are faced with the same difficulties today that the RAF was all those years ago. This was not a lack of tracking, quite the contrary. There were so many reports of unidentified aircraft that our limited fighter resources couldn't possibily respond to them all. Many of these sightings were made by AA batteries, whose aircraft recognition skills left a lot to be desired. Another problem was that the Firth of Forth was a busy training venue for all manner of aircraft, and the skies had been very busy that day. In particular, a number of Sea Skuas operating from RNAS Donibristle had been wrongly identified on a number of occasions, which had resulted in our Spitfires being sent away from the real enemy to investigate: one flight of Spitfires had even been sent to investigate, what turned out to be another flight of Spitfires.

Air Chief Marshal Dowding and the staff at Fighter Command Headquarters, who had watched the raid slowly build up, through the receipt of information from the radar chain, were well aware of the problems of tracking the enemy once they were over the mainland. Hugh Barkla, who was in the Stanmore Filter Room at the time of the raid told me:

'What went wrong was due to an over-reaction to a series of false alarms. The allocation of "hostile" identification to a track had been too lightly made, and the subsequent despatch of fighters to intercept had risked there being a shortage of fighters ready to deal with genuine raiders. The authority to name a track "hostile" was then restricted to too small a number of Controllers. With improvements in communications and in procedure in Movement Liaison, the number of unidentified tracks decreased, and the accuracy of identification of hostiles improved. It would have been remarkable if such a novel and complex system had not suffered some such swings.'

Another problem is the fact that the enemy didn't create a formation in the established sense, they crossed the coast over a widespread area. After the raid Air Chief Marshal Dowding himself admitted: 'The visibility conditions were difficult and the bomber formation split up into individual aircraft.' Andrew Jeffrey who is perhaps the leading authority on the raid having done years of research on the subject said: 'the truth of this story can be rather elusive. The formation was very scattered.'

I suppose the best person to ask would be the man who was leading the first wave of enemy aircraft. Helmut Pohle said: 'I came straight as an arrow from Westerland to the south coast of the Firth of Forth, just over the anchor place of the cruisers.'

According to Pohle, he flew straight towards the bridge, which was not what he had intended to do. His attack would therefore take place from the east, into the sun. Storp, approaching with the second wave would attack from the west, as planned.

Although there were a number of sightings reported by different sources around Dunbar, including a search-light crew who reported six Henschels at 1.25p.m. that turned out to be Sea Skuas from HMS *Merlin* at RNAS Donibristle, I think we can safely assume that at least some of these reports were accurate. Therefore, if Helmut Pohle and the first three Ju 88s had crossed the coast near Dunbar and were heading straight towards the Forth Bridge, their route would have taken them south of Drem near Haddington.

By this time Helmut Pohle would have made his first positive navigational fix. Through his Ordnance Survey map he would know that the nearby town was Dunbar; he would also know that Drem was ahead of him.

Pohle was exhilarated and this spread amongst his crew. The flight was going well. The difficult part of the navigational exercise was behind him. It had now become a visual flight. Looking over his shoulder Pohle could see less than a quarter of a mile away the second Junkers Ju 88. It rocked its wings momentarily indicating that all was well.

Pohle gently throttled back slightly and checked his altimeter. It was indicating ten thousand feet. Just about correct he thought to himself. Time, which only an hour ago had appeared to drag, now seemed to tick away at an incredible speed.

Where was the Royal Air Force?

Eye-witness David Watson was fourteen at the time and returning from Dunbar to Edinburgh with his parents. He said: 'We were at the summit of Pencraik Brae – part of the A1 between East Linton and Haddington when some planes appeared flying west. The sun roof of my father's Austin Ten was open and I recall standing up to get a better view. I could see the crosses on the aircraft. On our return to Edinburgh we learned of the raid.'

By this time the Ju 88s would have started to lose altitude, and would probably have been descending to around a planned altitude of 10,000 feet, and therefore increasingly visible from the ground; they would have to lose further altitude the closer they got to the target.

If it was Pohle's three aircraft that David Watson had seen, and they were still flying straight towards the bridge, they would next pass Tranent.

John Donaldson was nineteen at the time and living at Tranent, a village just to the south of Port Seton. Mr Donaldson wrote:

'Myself and a fellow employee of the Tranent Co-op were working in a field with a magnificent view of the Forth. We could make out the bridge in the distance.

'My attention was drawn to a lonely civil plane, which belonged, I think, to Edinburgh Flying Club. Suddenly it was joined up by a few heavier planes and instinctively I knew they were Gerrys. Fascinated, I wondered what the little plane would do, and to my astonishment and mirth, it gave them some sort of friendly salute.

'Suddenly it veered off as if like a shot rabbit looking for a hole to hide in. I guess we two young lads must have been the first persons to see the bombers. It has always been a mystery to me how they reached this far undetected.'

From Tranent, Helmut Pohle would have crossed the south shore of the Firth of Forth, and would have been heading up the river towards the Forth Bridge, which would have been quite visible to him by then. Inchkeith island in the centre of the river would have been off to his right, and again, in the Dunfermline Press account of the raid, eyewitnesses speak of three Ju 88s flying up-river past Inchkeith.

Eye-witness accounts are never completely reliable, and the Forth Raid provided dozens. Some eye-witness accounts quoted in the press contain enthralling accounts of huge four-engined aircraft, some painted red with a single black cross underneath! Echoes of von Richthofen no doubt.

At 2.27p.m. the commander of an anti-aircraft battery (RSG 1) in Dalmeny Park, just south of the Forth Bridge itself, reported the presence of three Ju 88s flying west at 10,000 feet. The battery had not received any sort of alarm or warning beforehand, so the sight of enemy aircraft came as a bit of a surprise. They had been practising loading blanks at the time. Their estimate of the height at which the aircraft were flying, may have been a little exaggerated, but their sighting gives us the final confirmation of Pohle's statement that he flew straight towards the bridge, up-river from the east.

The report made by the anti-aircraft battery at Dalmeny Park, was the first sighting of the enemy over the target area from an official source, by which time it was too late.

CHAPTER FIVE

BOMBS OVER BRITAIN

On 16 October 1939 the first Nazi bombs began to fall over Britain at approximately 2.30p.m. Just prior to this a Naval signal was issued saying: 'Air raid over the Firth of Forth. All aircraft to be regarded as friendly, unless proved hostile.' Could mean anything really, couldn't it?

Helmut Pohle with the first three aircraft had arrived over the target area. He was heading straight towards the Forth Bridge, just beyond which was the Royal Navy base at Rosyth. His eyes searched across the surface of the water for any sign of the battleship HMS *Hood*. However, apart from some small vessels lying off the dockyard nothing of any importance could be seen in the water. It was then that he noticed – still some way off in the distance – the great vessel they had studied so long to destroy. Yet through another twist of fate, she was out of their reach. The *Hood* was already in dock. The frustration must have been immense. They had flown over 500 crippling miles, to be denied their prize. The temptation to ignore their orders and attack the *Hood* regardless, must have crossed all their minds. Helmut Pohle was not the sort of man who would disobey a direct order, so HMS *Hood* was safe. On the near side of the Forth Bridge he could see the two cruisers, HMS *Southampton* and HMS *Edinburgh*. The trio of Ju 88s continued straight towards the bridge and their secondary targets, with bomb doors open.

The time was 2.27p.m., only three minutes until the first bombs would straddle the Royal Navy vessels.

Helmut Pohle remembered the exact moment of his attack very well:

'When I arrived over the Firth of Forth in my Ju 88 I could see the *Hood* already in the dock of Rosyth. However, in the Firth lay HMS *Southampton* and HMS *Edinburgh* at anchor. I attacked as the first of twelve Ju 88s the *Southampton*. But during the dive the top part of the canopy came off. Although after the dive-attack I was now flying with my crew in a half-open plane, I nevertheless remained in the area to observe the results of the other aircraft.

'After the dive-attack from 12,000 feet to 1,800 feet, when I released the bombs, I continued down to 900 feet. I turned right and flew outside the famous bridge to the north coast of the Firth of Forth.'

Helmut Pohle's last statement again confirms two important points, the direction of his attack and the height at which he approached the dive. The initial dive was instigated from some considerable height, and as he turned right after the attack, which took him north, he had attacked up-river from the east.

Sigmund Storp who was approaching Rosyth with the second wave of bombers had made a very different approach. His route had taken him to the south of Edinburgh.

He had crossed the coast to the north of Berwick-on-Tweed and in less than five minutes, with all eyes quartering the sky for enemy fighters the bomb-aimer called out that the village of Lauder was coming up under the nose. Another seven or eight minutes and they should see the large reservoir at Gladhouse.

Storp was aware of his crew coming to action stations. He didn't need to tell them, such was the unspoken understanding between the four.

Far off to his right he could see the Firth of Forth and even the top of the Forth railway bridge. Another five minutes or so would see them over their turning point, Threipmuir, the long elongated reservoir on the north side of the Pentland Hills.

He could see it now, quite clearly, dead ahead. Incredibly, there was still no sign of any interception from the RAF. He was only minutes away from the target. Storp deliberately throttled back and lowered the nose. He searched in vain for Turnhouse, for any sight of activity either on the ground or in the air.

Over the Threipmuir Reservoir he began to turn his aircraft to make a wide sweep over Rosyth. His flight, and the third flight of aircraft following behind, had gone exactly to plan. They would attack Rosyth from the south-west with the sun at their back. After their attack they would already be heading east along the Firth of Forth and home.

Falling in line with Storp's account, is a report made by PC James Henderson from the Police Station at Roslin. Roslin lies to the south of Edinburgh on the approach to the Threipmuir Reservoir. Not only does this put the aircraft in the right place, but he also stated that they were flying at a very high altitude in a westerly direction; which of course they still would have been at that time – 2.35p.m. The AA Battery at Dalmeny Park had estimated Pohle's approach at 10,000 feet, and Pohle himself said that before the dive he was at 12,000 feet. Quite possibly, both of these heights have been slighty overestimated. Storp, with the second wave of bombers would hit the target at 2.38p.m.

Like Helmut Pohle, Sigmund Storp remembered his approach very well:

> 'Suddenly we sighted the coast. We turned inland to approach the bridge from the west. Now it becomes a question of attack, each machine by itself. I have the sun at my back. Nothing is to be seen of any anti-aircraft defences. But where is the *Hood*? To our disgust she was in dry dock, and by Führer's orders, there must be no bombs dropped on land. So the *Hood* is safe from us.'

What the Germans didn't realise at the time was that the battleship they had orders to bomb and which they had studied intensely before the raid, was in fact HMS *Repulse*, not HMS *Hood*. Reconnaissance aircraft had followed the *Repulse* some time earlier and she had been mistaken for her sister ship the *Hood*. Their similarities were great indeed, but once again this mistake helps to illustrate the inadequacies of German intelligence. Storp went on:

> 'But in front of the big bridge in the Firth of Forth, I espied a few boats. I tell the others over the radio, "We attack!" Then I put the plane's nose down, and take a ship into my sights. So down to 2,500 feet goes the dive, and I slowly recognise that I have a cruiser in my sights. Later I heard that it was the *Southampton*. And still no anti-aircraft defence. At 2,400 feet I let my two bombs loose. Slowly I bring the machine out of the dive, but I still go down to about 800 feet. We see that our bombs have hit the cruiser.'

It's difficult to know which of the German aircraft bombed which vessel. However we do know from Sigmund Storp, he was confident that his charges were aimed at the cruiser *Southampton*. One bomb glanced off the cruiser, causing slight damage near her bow, and sank the Admiral's barge and pinnace which were moored empty alongside. Apparently the bomb had passed through the cruiser's port hangar and the boy seamen's messdeck before emerging through the hull just above the waterline, where the eventual explosion took place. There were three casualties on board the *Southampton*, and seven casualties on board the cruiser *Edinburgh*; none of which were fatal.

These were ships of the 2nd Cruiser Squadron commanded by Vice-Admiral Sir Edward Collins. The damage and injuries could have been a lot worse. HMS *Southampton* had survived by the skin of her teeth, rather like a bullet passing straight through a soldier's body, missing all the vital organs and leaving him with nothing more than a gaping hole and excruciating pain.

Hauptmann Helmut Pohle was quite adamant that his bombs had also been aimed at HMS *Southampton*. After dropping his own bombs Pohle circled over Inverkeithing Bay enabling himself to observe the second wave of bombers come in at 2.38p.m., which included Sigmund Storp. Although he hasn't actually said so himself, I imagine that Pohle was also using his aircraft to mark the target. By this time the anti-aircraft battery at Dalmeny Park was the first into action. Others in the vicinity opened up shortly afterwards.

Even though the Battery at Dalmeny Park had reported the first enemy planes at 2.27p.m., it had taken eleven minutes before they were given the order to open fire. The unfortunate crew had to sit and watch the bombers swoop down and attack the Royal Navy, right before their eyes for several minutes, before their superiors gave them permission to open up.

Mr A. Neilson, who had been in the RAF himself, was an eye-witness to the whole thing from a position very close to the Battery at Dalmeny Park. He wrote at the time:

'On Monday, October 16, at 2.30p.m., my wife and I chanced to be travelling slowly along a coast road on the Firth of Forth, at a point exactly opposite two cruisers, *Edinburgh* and the *Southampton*.

'Suddenly there was a loud cracking noise which seemed to be within the car, and which I immediately diagnosed as a broken ball-race. Again! But this time the cracking noise was a few hundred yards away and easily recognisable as machine-gun fire. I stopped the car and jumped out just in time to see a great volume of water shoot up within a few yards of one of the cruisers. "Air Raid!" I called. "Come out quick!"

'The attacker had gone, but presently the cruisers started loosing their shells to a height of about 6,000 feet. Up among the white puffs of smoke my wife spotted something. "Look, there he is!" As she spoke the machine banked and came down in a fast dive from the west. Down, down he came, until directly over the Forth Bridge he released two large bombs whose course we were able to follow until they plunged into the river within a few yards of one of the cruisers.

'Several times this happened, and of the bombs which were dropped I should say more than one was as near as thirty yards from one or other of the cruisers. Certainly a lucky day for them. Right behind us in a wood an anti-aircraft battery blazed away, and as we were not more than 400 yards from the cruisers the noise was terrific, and all about us we could hear quite distinctly the orders given on the ship's loud-speakers.

'As we were on rising ground and looking down on the scene we had a perfect view of the whole affair. My wife was a bit afraid to begin with, but I insisted that we were tremendously fortunate to get such a view and that we might never have such an opportunity again. I may say it was fairly obvious she was satisfied on this point – but not just in the way I intended her to be. I continued to reassure her, however, and pointed out that there was not a chance in a million of a bomb dropping near us as the marksmanship was far too good for that. The danger of shrapnel dropping on us was slight as we were too close to the guns. One large piece did, however, land within fifty yards of my car. What I did not tell her and what I dared not think about was my secret fear of what would have happened to us if one of the bombs had made a lucky hit where the raider was aiming.

'It was a most thrilling experience which I should not have missed for a great deal.'

Mr Neilson's vivid account was published in *The War Illustrated* on 18 November 1939. Another eye witness was Mr Peter Walker, Provost of South Queensferry, who watched the raid from his house two miles away.

'I heard a terrific explosion, and saw a great waterspout rising from the river into the air.

'A bomb was released, and I could plainly see it fall.

'More planes came over. A terrible hail of shells went up from the anti-aircraft batteries.

'It seemed as though the raiding aircraft reeled. Then they seemed to recover. Numbers of bombs fell – but all dropped into the water.

'It seemed impossible that the planes could live in the barrage of shrapnel put up by the anti-aircraft guns. A shot struck one plane and I saw part of the machine fall into the Firth.

'Our guns seemed to be aimed quite coolly, though I counted about twenty bombs when the raiders first swooped down. The planes were beaten off for a time but back they came, apparently determined to bomb the Forth Bridge.

'It was only after the first bombs had been dropped that I heard an air raid siren go. Just as I heard it I saw a single German plane coming across the river.

'I heard a number of terrific explosions, but so far as I could see no damage was done. Anti-aircraft fire forced this machine to retire. After a few minutes of this amazingly hot attack and equally active defence a number of speedy British fighters streaked over in pursuit of the Germans.'

Mr Walker's account talks of the Germans leaving the area after dropping their bombs and returning a short time later. As the raiders had only two bombs each, after they had dropped them, apart from Helmut Pohle who circled overhead, the Germans headed home. What Mr Walker saw was the approach of the subsequent bombers.

After each of the Ju 88s had flown over the target and released their bombs, they were already heading towards the east. The idea was to fly directly along the Firth of Forth, as quickly as possible and head for the North Sea and home.

Mr Walker also heard an air raid siren sound. Evidence of this somewhat delicate issue, which you shall read later, shows that no public warnings were given to the public in or around Edinburgh at any time during the raid. They did sound in military establishments. What Mr Walker heard was undoubtedly the siren at the Royal Navy base at Port Edgar, which is situated next to South Queensferry where he lived.

James Clark was an apprentice in the building trade working in the Royal Navy establishment at Port Edgar near South Queensferry on the south side of the Forth; directly under the final approach to the target, of the second and third waves of raiders. He was working at Port Edgar on the refurbishment of accommodation for naval personnel. He recalls:

'On that morning there was some aerial activity. I remember the journeyman I was working with asking me what type of aircraft it was, being eighteen he thought I would know, I did say it was a Blenheim, but how wrong I was! Later it was acknowledged to be a German reconnaissance aircraft – a Heinkel.'

The aircraft which Mr Clark had seen was one of the two Heinkels from Westerland that had flown over the target area that morning. Pinkerton had of course, intercepted an intruder at 10.15a.m. near Dunbar, which had evaded him by escaping into the clouds.

Mr Clark goes on to say:

'Early in the afternoon things began to warm up. Suddenly there was the sound of gunfire; this came from the anti-aircraft batteries. Then the sound of sirens. On looking up we saw two planes flying over the bridge with the puffs of bursting shells following them. I remember everybody on the site had gathered out in the open and were cheering the gunners as these shells burst closer and closer. None of us ever having been in an air raid before, we didn't appreciate the danger: we soon did, when a naval officer bore down on us, with a big lump of jagged metal in his hand and politely told us to get into the bloody shelter. Gerry didn't stop for very long. After we got the all-clear we went back to work. On finishing work we had to walk past the base hospital, there we saw them removing the wounded who had been brought in from the ships that were in the Firth of Forth at the time of the raid. I have often wondered what Gerry's target was, the bridge or the ships, or both. I believe the Germans published photographs of the railway bridge having been hit by a bomb. Actually they had turned the photograph upside down and the puff of smoke from the bursting bomb was really Inch Garvie island which supports one of the piers.'

The official police report which was made by Inspector Maclean from South Queensferry Police Station on the day of the raid, stated:

'I beg to report that an Enemy Air Raid commenced about 2.30p.m. on this date (16 October 1939) over the Firth of Forth in the vicinity of the Forth Bridge, where HMS *Edinburgh* and HMS *Southampton* were at anchor a short distance east of the Bridge and south of Inch Garvie Island. Four attacks were made on the warships by three enemy aeroplanes, ten or twelve bombs being dropped between the ships and the Forth Bridge. Two small boats tied to HMS *Edinburgh* were damaged and sunk and so far as is known there was one casualty on that ship, a naval rating being seriously wounded. No bombs dropped on land, at least within this county, but shrapnel fell at the Town Harbour, South Queensferry (in the sea), on Hawes Brae and at Newgardens House, Dalmeny. Shrapnel also fell at the house occupied by David Drummond, Water Superintendent, Queensferry Road, Kirkliston, and Peter McGowan (24), farmer of Wheatlands Farm, Kirkliston was slightly wounded on the back by shrapnel while working in a field on that farm.'

It's interesting to note that Inspector Maclean, in accordance with many other people, thought the entire raid was carried out by only three aircraft. They didn't appear to realise at the time that there were several waves of raiders. The fact that Helmut Pohle had been observed by many sources, circling the target area, must have given the people on the ground the impression, that after each dive the same aircraft had circled and attacked again; whereas in actual fact, after each attack, the other Ju 88s had all made for home.

To the east of the bridge and right in the centre of the Firth of Forth lies Inchkeith island, which would have been directly under the flight path of the Ju 88s as they headed for the sea. A detachment of the 7/9 Royal Scots Regiment happened to be on the island, among them Jas Ross. The detachment's duty on the island was to patrol 24 hours a day, as Mr Ross explains:

A pre-war photograph of 603 Squadron groundcrew at Turnhouse. Mr G. Mullay, standing second from right. *(Photograph courtesy of George Mullay)*

603 Squadron 'A' Flight in early 1940. *Left to Right - seated:* Flying Officer J. G. E. Haig, Flight Lieutenant G. L. Denholm, Squadron Leader E. H. Stevens, Flying Officer H. K. Macdonald, Flying Officer Alen Wallace. *Standing:* Sergeant J. R. Caister, Flying Officer Ian Ritchie, Flying Officer J. Morton, Pilot Officer G. Gilroy, Pilot Officer P. O. Barton and Warrant Officer J. Dalziel. *(Photograph courtesy of Andrew Jeffrey)*

Patsy Gifford on the ground at Turnhouse stands in front of Spitfire XT-A
(Stickleback), the first Spitfire to shoot down an enemy aircraft in combat. The
photograph is said to have been taken during the afternoon of 16 October 1939.
(Photograph courtesy of Andrew Jeffrey)

603 Squadron groundcrew refuel a Spitfire at Turnhouse. Standing on the wing is Mr G. Mullay. Note the letter 'A' on the arm of the sergeant, denoting 'Auxiliary'.

(Photograph courtesy of George Mullay)

Men of the Royal Army Ordnance Corps who manned Lewis guns at Stirling on 16 October 1939. Third from left James Cranston. *(Photograph courtesy of Mr J. Cranston)*

The replica Spitfire at RAF Turnhouse which bears the markings of Patsy Gifford's L1070 (XT-A). *(Photograph courtesy of Brian Farish)*

'We had to pick our way around the rocks and descend a steep rock formation, by means of steps known as Jacob's Ladder. This patrol consisted of
two pairs of soldiers going each way, and we would pop into the various gun
emplacements on the island, which were 18-inch guns guarding the entrance
to the Firth of Forth.'

In the afternoon the paddle steamer had arrived with stores. Some of
the soldiers were helping to unload. Mr Ross recalls:

'Whilst lifting a cardboard box containing large round silver tins of meat
loaf, three of the tins rolled over the side of the ship when the bottom of the
box burst. At that particular time a German bomber flew overhead. The
result was that soldiers leaning over the ship rails below awaiting shore-leave
to Leith, saw the flash of tins going into the harbour at the same time as the
bomber flew overhead. There was a rush for safety. Many wearing gas-
masks clambered upstairs on to the main deck saying that bombs had fallen.
For myself I had left the box, in case I was held responsible for the loss of
rations. I feel sure many of these soldiers were still convinced that an attack
had been made on the paddle steamer.

'There were no anti-aircraft guns on the island and as far as I am aware
no shots were fired at the aircraft during the raid. The Royal Scots were
stationed in Fife where we were sent at the outbreak of war, when mobilised
as Territorials on 28 August 1939.'

Up until this point, except for belated anti-aircraft bursts and the
return of fire from the cruisers, the raiders were able to do as they
pleased unchallenged. Incredibly, the Royal Air Force had still not
arrived on the scene.

George Pinkerton led his section towards Dalkeith; Archie McKellar
on his right, Paul Webb on his left. The weather was still fairly good –
woolly, broken cloud over land at about 4,000 feet, good visibility otherwise. Over the R/T he received a message from Controller: 'Investigate
two unidentified aircraft over Tranent, Angel Two.' A few moments
later he reported that he could see nothing except three Spitfires going
in to land at Drem (this was Red Section returning from their patrol over
Crail). His message was immediately answered. 'Enemy aircraft
bombing Rosyth. Patrol five miles north of present position.' The time
was 2.30p.m. A group of German bombers (local estimates – twelve in
all) had swept down on the Forth Bridge and the first air raid on mainland Britain had started.

In the Ops Room at Turnhouse there was feverish excitement. Top
brass came crowding in (unnecessarily) to see what was going on. The

Controller, Bob Johnstone, immediately ordered Yellow Section of 603 Squadron up (consisting of Flight Lieutenant George Denholm, Pilot Officer 'Sheep' Gilroy, and Pilot Officer Jim 'Black' Morton). According to the Squadron's Operations Record Book, Yellow Section's time up was 2.35p.m.

A few miles south of Turnhouse lies the Threipmuir Reservoir, where Yellow Section, barely off the runway and still climbing, found their paths being crossed by three invaders. Threipmuir Reservoir, as we pointed out earlier had been used by the Germans as the point from which they would begin to bank north-east for their attack, so it is therefore quite obvious that the three aircraft which crossed the path of Yellow Section were still on their approach to Rosyth. The time was 2.35p.m., the exact moment that Storp had passed over Threipmuir. It is therefore evident that the three Ju 88s that crossed the path of George Denholm's section as they took off from Turnhouse, were those of Sigmund Storp and Co.

Red Section of 602, newly-landed at Drem, were feverishly refuelled and stood by in their aircraft. News of the flap spread fast. The word spread round, 'THIS IS IT'. Pilots came running over to the Flight Hut at Drem, where Cairns Smith could scarcely hear himself talk for pilots breathing down his neck excitedly and trying to hear the telephone messages simultaneously. In the general confusion, he forgot to note the orders and times in the squadron log-book. The news even reached the dentist's hut and Flying Officer Finlay Boyd sprang gratefully from the chair and went running over to dispersal.

At Turnhouse dispersal, Patsy Gifford fumed impatiently as George Denholm and Yellow Section took off. He grabbed a phone and started badgering Ops Room to allow him to take a section up. The station commander, Wing Commander Donald Fleming, gave his permission. Gifford raced for his Spitfire, and led Red Section off towards the Forth Bridge (this section consisted of Gifford, Flying Officer Ken Macdonald, and Pilot Officer Colin (Robbie) Robertson). Within minutes, six sections of Spitfires, spearheaded by Pinkerton and Denholm, with Gifford coming up fast behind, were in the air on their way to intercept.

At Turnhouse, as with the other airfields in the vicinity, the sirens had sent everyone scuttling to the air raid shelters. James Marshall, who still lives in Edinburgh today, was an auxiliary airman with 603 Squadron at the time. He told me: 'I remember the day well as it was the only time I spent in an air raid shelter during the entire war.'

Squadron Leader the Reverend J. Rossie Brown, 603 Squadron's padre, was just beginning his drive into Edinburgh, to visit Pilot Officer Hunter in the military hospital, when the sound of the siren stopped him dead in his tracks. He got out the car and rushed to his machine-gun post. Turnhouse was a mere three and a half miles south of Dalmeny Park, at the southern end of the Forth Railway Bridge. The padre and the other gunners at the station 'had a fine view of the Bosche dive-bombing towards the Forth.' They could clearly see the puffs of smoke as AA shells burst around the bombers, and Spitfires rushed to the fray.

At South Queensferry at 2.30p.m. on that afternoon, passers-by were idly enjoying the mild autumn weather when they suddenly saw planes swooping down from the west. AA batteries started up as the first bombs landed with spouts of water near the warships anchored off Rosyth. A Naval Swordfish from RNAS Donibristle in Fife, innocently practising bombing in the Forth estuary off Aberdour, suddenly found itself in the midst of swooping Ju 88s and flak bursts, and hastened home in panic.

Jas Cessford recalls:

'I was on a business trip to Fife from Edinburgh and had just joined the car ferry at Hawes Pier, South Queensferry, when the attack on HMS *Edinburgh* took place.

'The car ferry crew wanted us to take the cars off – Lord alone knows why! We retreated to the door of the Hawes Inn to watch what was going on. The doors to this public house had just been closed by the proprietor and they rattled as the bombing took place.

'The flight path of the attack was from the south-west side of the Forth as I remember it; with the Germans moving north-east towards HMS *Edinburgh* which lay just to the east of the Forth Bridge. The results of the bombing attack were all near misses, and I thought at the time that the German pilots could not make up their minds whether to hit the bridge or the cruiser.

'As the raid continued a commercial traveller drove up to the Hawes Inn from Edinburgh, got out of his car and demanded to know why the pub was closed when it should have been open, as he was gasping for a pint. We Scots are pretty douce!

'Incidentally, I got called-up and joined the Royal Navy, and learned just how quickly "action stations" could be implemented. In the case of HMS *Edinburgh*, I thought that she was extremely slow to return fire on that day.'

Also taken from the ferry at Hawes Pier was the Cowdenbeath ambulance; the patients from which were given tea by a Voluntary Aid Detachment in a nearby shelter.

One of the most incredible things about the raid is the fact that while it was going on, trains were allowed to cross the Forth Railway Bridge. Alex Farish – then thirty-nine years of age – worked for the L.N.E.R. company and was on duty with a colleague in the control office at

Waverley Station, when a telephone call came through from the signalman in the box at Forth Bridge North saying that there were German bombers all over the place. His son Brian, who was five in 1939, told me:

'This particular signalbox was located on the north approach viaduct to the Forth Bridge high above the village of North Queensferry. Bear in mind that at this time no air raid sirens had sounded in the Edinburgh area, although the raid had already been in force for many minutes. At the time of the call there was probably about eight or nine controllers on duty each responsible for the running of trains on different sections of line. The immediate reaction was to doubt the sanity of the signalman concerned and this point was made to him in no uncertain terms. The question of alcohol was also raised.

'On the point of hanging up the telephone the signalman opened up a sliding window in the signalbox and said that if nobody in Edinburgh believed him they were just to listen to the bedlam that was going on right above the Forth Bridge.

'The sound of anti-aircraft fire, exploding bombs and aircraft could be clearly heard. By this time the remaining staff in the control were clustered around the position of the controller responsible for the Edinburgh to Inverkeithing section of line.

'At this time a far more important decision had to be taken, and that concerned the safety of passengers on board the 2.30p.m. Edinburgh to Dunfermline train which had stopped at Dalmeny Station and was then ready to proceed over the Forth Bridge.

'After some hurried consultation it was agreed to let the train run – after all the sirens had still not sounded and there was just the chance that this was only a major exercise!

'Fear of the railway bosses if the train was delayed was probably greater than fear of what the Luftwaffe might do. And so a train-load of passengers was allowed to cross the bridge in the middle of the first enemy air raid on mainland Britain. Lady luck rode that train that sunny October afternoon.

'For another half hour, nobody, except the harrassed signalman at Forth Bridge North was entirely convinced about what was happening . . . until, that is, another telephone rang this time from the Burntisland control office located in a building at the side of the Forth some seven miles down river from the Forth Bridge.

'A member of the Burntisland office staff had seen a German bomber, complete with black cross, trailing smoke and being chased by a Spitfire flying down the Forth towards Kirkcaldy. He said, "Didn't the silly B . . . . s in Edinburgh realise that there was a major air raid in progress over the Forth and why were trains still being allowed to cross the Forth Bridge." All hell broke loose – and the L.N.E.R. went to war!'"

A photograph, taken from one of the enemy aircraft was published upside-down in a Berlin illustrated newspaper, and purported to show a bomb bursting on the Forth Bridge. The clearly visible bomb explosion, which took place to the left of the centre pier, was, in reality, Inch Garvie Island upon which the pier was built.

One of the passengers on the train was Christine Dingwall from Kirkcaldy. She was just nineteen and training to be a teacher at Moray House Training College, Edinburgh. Her sister Jessica still lives in Kirkcaldy, and told me 'I was at home with my mother when the intimation came over the radio. I remember my Mother standing stock-still'.

Another passenger interviewed at the time said: 'At Dalmeny we were informed that an air raid was in progress, and it was left to our own discretion whether we would continue the journey across the Forth Bridge. Most of us decided to continue. As the train travelled slowly across the bridge we were able to watch the progress of the raid. Two aeroplanes, one near the south shore and one to the north shore of the Forth, appeared to dive over the bridge, and bombs were dropped a short distance to the east of the bridge. A great column of water shot up.' Another eye-witness also stated: 'I saw three or four aeroplanes. They dropped about ten bombs, but all hit the water. I saw raiders come up three times, with about half an hour between. They were fairly high. They were shelled by our defences.'

Miss Hunter from Charlestown, who was a student at Moray House Training College, said that when the bombs exploded in the water the steelwork of the bridge seemed to vibrate from top to bottom.

James Clark, who you will recall was working at the Royal Navy base at Port Edgar during the raid, told me: 'My cousin who was a submariner was in the train which had left Edinburgh for Rosyth and was on the bridge when the raid was in progress, he did say it was quite an experience.'

The consensus of opinion is that while the first attack took place the train was delayed at Dalmeny, where passengers were allowed to take shelter if so desired. After the attack, it was decided to let the train proceed. Just as the train set forth, the second wave of bombers appeared on the scene. Mr Carter, an Edinburgh commercial traveller, and passenger on the train was reported to say at the time:

'Anti-aircraft fire opened up, and bombs were dropped, but nowhere near the ships, except one, which fell right at the side of one of them.

There was terrific spray and we thought at first that it had been hit.

'We were allowed to proceed, but more planes came over. We were on the bridge when the last bomb was dropped. The train went slowly, and the planes were swooping overhead.

'The bombing was concentrated on the larger ship. The attackers had a very hot reception.'

I must admit that I have tried and failed in an attempt to track down the actual number of the engine that crossed the bridge at the time. It was almost certainly a 'Scott' class 4-4-0 locomotive, 1914 design.

The fact that the Germans were able to attempt three separate attacks on the ships over a period of time, only goes to emphasise the unusually slow response that was made by the Air Force. The Nazi pilots had intended to approach and attack undetected, and gain a victory through surprise. I expect that even they were astonished by the freedom with which they were allowed to carry on attacking the ships, seemingly at their leisure. Their only problem during the bombing itself came from the anti-aircraft positions on the ground and some from the ships.

Indeed, thrice the bombers swooped and struck, dropping forty bombs in all (Air Ministry figure). On retrospect, although a Ju 88 was capable of carrying a far bigger load, during the Forth Raid they were only fitted with two bombs each. Both Helmut Pohle and Sigmund Storp, as well as other sources have confirmed this fact. This means that if all twelve aircraft had dropped their charges over the target area, there would have been a maximum of twenty-four bombs. At least one of the aircraft did not drop his bombs over the target area, and was to use them a little later with devastating consequences.

Also note that most official, and eye-witness accounts, talk of three attacks over the target area. This only accounts for nine aircraft. The last wave of aircraft, had drifted some distance north, which made their subsequent arrival on the scene some time later. We can therefore almost, look at the last wave separately, and consider that the main attack on the prescribed target area was carried out by the first three waves of Ju 88s, between 2.30p.m. and 3.00p.m. Inspector Maclean's report from South Queensferry Police Station said that 'Four attacks were made on the warships.' He may well include in this calculation the last bombers to be seen over the target area which he put at 'about 4pm.' This would have been the final aircraft, and from this report alone we can tell that they were a good hour behind the others.

As the Ju 88s pulled away from the third attack and scattered for home, the Spitfires began to converge on the scene. The chase was on!

CHAPTER SIX

FIRST BLOOD TO THE
AUXILIARIES

O *berleutnant* Sigmund Storp, who was about to become the first
German pilot to be shot down over Britain during the Second
World War, vividly remembered the exact moment that the
enemy arrived to upset his game:

'Then I commit my biggest mistake. I climb. Suddenly, out of a serene
sky, machine-guns fire at us. My co-pilot calls out, terrified, "Spitfires behind
us!" But the first spatter of bullets had hit us. My left engine was out of action.
I took violent evasive action. Ten to twelve Spitfires were after me. I
resemble a hare shot and wounded, but still chased. My gunner had been
killed in the first burst. I pressed my bird down. To get away was our only
thought. But the Spitfires curved around us like devils. One burst after the
other made a sieve of our Ju.

'The hell-like flight went right over the roofs of Edinburgh. Here we had
respite for some seconds. The British did not shoot when over the city. My
only thought was that the machine should not go down on land: it should
not fall into enemy hands. I steered towards the sea. Where had the British
hunters come from so quickly? Why had we not spotted them earlier? These
were the thoughts that kept me busy while I was steering. My bird was
finished. At about 700 feet the elevators went out of action. The machine
capsized, nose forward, and fell into the sea like a stone. In the last second
I was able to throw off the roof of the cockpit.

'I was thrown about 70 yards, still fastened to my seat. I came to under
water, swam to the surface.'

Storp described how he and the two crew survivors were saved by a
Scottish fisherman. 'I gave him a signet ring.' Storp said a news-reel film of
his capture was shown in a Stockholm cinema, and seen by a girl acquain-
tance – who sent a cable to Germany, where he was assumed to be dead.

The Ju 88 flown by *Oberleutnant* Sigmund Storp (Ju 88 – 4D + DH) was the first German aircraft to be shot down over Britain during the Second World War. It flopped into the Forth's cold October waters just north of Port Seton at 2.45p.m.

Patsy Gifford's own account of Storp's final moments were reproduced in a little booklet published in aid of the inauguration of the squadron's benevolent fund in 1943. As Gifford was killed in the Spring of 1940 it was printed sometime after his death. However, shortly after the raid Gifford was visited at Turnhouse by A. Scott Kennedy, Aeronautical Correspondent of *The Scotsman*. Kennedy had been a familiar figure to the squadron long before the war, and had always shown a keen interest in their activities. He was invited for a drink in the Mess and in order to escape the banter in the ante-room, Gifford invited him upstairs to his bedroom. He was privileged to be the only journalist present, which was just as well, as it was a very small room, with just one bed and no chairs to sit on. Kennedy noted the room's accoutrements, which very much fall in line with the sporting character we know Gifford to have been; 'there were sporting gun-cases, a squash racquet or two, and some fencing foils filled the corners.' They squatted on the bed and talked. According to Kennedy, Gifford came across as extremely modest to begin with, and although a solicitor in his civilian life, he preferred to sit back and let the journalist do all the talking. That was exactly what Kennedy didn't want to do, and although 'line shooting' was not encouraged in the service, he pointed out that 'Edinburgh, Scotland, the whole country, indeed the whole world,' was interested in knowing the facts: not to mention Herr Göring! Gradually Gifford began to open up and a story pieced together.

'Well' he said, with a cheerful laugh, 'I'm glad for two reasons – (a) for the Squadron's sake, and (b) I've won my bet.' Red section had taken off at 2.30p.m. and at 2.55p.m. had landed back at base with the first Nazi 'in the bag.' Twenty-five minutes from the time of take-off to landing and the job was done.

Gifford's account put them at 3,000 feet. Visibility was not specially good, as there was an autumn haze between them and the ground. 'Things were shimmering a bit.' Overhead were big patches of heavy cloud with clear sky lanes between. 'Look out there's a twin-engined job to starboard,' he heard his No 2 call on the radio telephone. Almost immediately an enemy bomber appeared out of a cloud. He was flying fast, heading straight towards them; head on! Evidently spotting them, the German swung off into a handy patch of cloud, but not before his guns had attempted to rake the approaching fighters.

Red Leader spoke a few words over the R/T and threw his machine into a stiff climbing turn. The others followed tightly.

'He dived away, and I stayed above him long enough to make certain that he was a Hun. There was no doubt of his markings. Then I went down in a stiff dive, came up under his tail. He filled the gun-sight, and I let drive before pulling out. Perhaps I was a bit too close, but there he was. I gave him a long burst.

'He was responding with all his armament; tracers were shooting past me, and I got a glimpse of a gunner behind twin guns. We went in again and gave him some more, and I saw he was hit forward. Bits of fabric were dropping off, and I thought I saw a red glow inside the fuselage.

'I broke away as his guns flashed again. At that moment one of my chaps came in at speed with his eight firing. We were now over the coast and as the German sought a lower course, we simply sprayed him with bullets. I could see our fire furrowing the water.'

Then came the end. The German was badly crippled. The rear-gunner was silent.

'As soon as the Spitfire in front of me had broken away after giving him another burst, I went close in and gave him all I had.

'He flopped in the sea, and as we circled overhead we saw he was sinking. One man was swimming and some boats were approaching. We returned to our station, and after refuelling and re-arming, took off again.'

Gifford's bet by the way, was that he would be the first pilot of 603 Squadron to shoot down an enemy aircraft. I expect the manner in which he did it, not to mention the prestigious occasion, surprised even him.

When Patsy Gifford had first encountered Sigmund Storp's aircraft, it was already being fired upon by Pilot Officer Jim Morton. Morton, in Yellow Section, had met three Germans at the Forth Bridge. You may recall that Yellow Section led by George Denholm had taken off from Turnhouse, at the same time that Storp's three aircraft has passed over the Threipmuir Reservoir. Yellow Section had split up into individual attacks. Morton engaged his prey (Storp) over Colinton and chased him east. 'I think I killed the rear gunner and knocked out the port engine. He started to lose height, and when we were just over Wallyford, Gifford's section arrived.'

Morton had emptied his guns, and now returned home. Gifford and his two colleagues attacked repeatedly, as Storp ducked and turned.

They crossed the coast off Port Seton; Storp was losing height, bits of fabric were dropping from his plane; bullets were furrowing the sea as the Spitfires closed. Gifford made one last attack and emptied his remaining guns into the crippled German, which flopped into the sea. A fishing vessel nearby hurried over and picked up Storp and two others of the crew as the plane sank. Storp's rear gunner *Obergefreiter* Kramer was the only member of the crew who was not rescued; most probably, as Jim Morton supposes, he was already dead before the plane crashed into the water.

Gifford's section hurried back to Turnhouse to refuel. The leading section was also on the ground by this time. But Flight Lieutenant George Denholm had come in too fast and ended up in the soft muddy ground at the far end of the runway; his machine stuck fast, and was being manhandled out by an Army squad. Pilot Officer 'Sheep' Gilroy's plane had been struck, a bullet passing through the top of the engine cover, and was being inspected. Gilroy's aircraft (L.1048) was therefore, the first Spitfire to sustain battle damage; although very minor. Pilot Officer Jim Morton, the junior pilot, was waiting to be refuelled and re-armed when Gifford's three touched down and demanded first attention. They were made ready at tremendous speed, the ground-crews working absolutely flat out, and took off again – leaving Morton fuming impatiently on the ground.

The last few moments of Storp's wartime career as a brilliant pilot were observed from the ground by Thos Stewart, who remembers:

'It so happens that on that particular day I witnessed the shooting down of a German bomber by two British fighter aircraft. At that time I was living in Prestonpans which is more or less next door to Cockenzie & Port Seton, and had just left my landlady's house when I heard the sound of aircraft and machine-gun fire. Looking round, I saw three aircraft, one a German bomber and two RAF fighters both of which were raking the bomber with bullets. The aircraft passed almost directly overhead and there was some smoke coming from the bomber which was not travelling at a high speed. It seemed to me as if the pilot wanted to avoid crashing on land and to come down in the sea as near the shoreline as possible. Although I was on an elevated part of Prestonpans and had a wide view over shore and sea I was just too far away to get all the details. But small boats did go out to the aircraft and soon after an ambulance and police arrived. There might have been casualties but I did not hear of any fatalities.'

John Donaldson, the young man of nineteen, who had been working in a field at Tranent, and who had seen Helmut Pohle's three Ju 88s on their way to the raid, was another eye-witness to Storp's crash into the Forth.

Mr Donaldson remembers the aircraft being chased by several Spitfires, and its eventual crash onto the sea about half a mile out. He was also aware that a fisherman who had rescued the pilot of the stricken aircraft had boasted that he had given him a gold ring. The truth of this story has already been proven to us by Storp himself who admitted that he had given the man a signet ring.

'The bombers were being hotly pursued by fighters' he wrote, 'low flying and blasting away with machine-guns. I had an excellent view of the one shot down into the sea off Port Seton. Another flew over our heads making for the hills with spent bullets hitting the shed behind us.'

No air raid sirens – except for those in the military establishments – sounded in Edinburgh that afternoon for some unaccountable reason (although they had sounded on the first day of the war when an unidentified aircraft was spotted over the English Channel). The people of Edinburgh first realised there was something on when they heard the noise of anti-aircraft guns firing to the north, and saw the Spitfires sweeping overhead. A few minutes later, many of them were to get worm's-eye views of some of the individual dogfights with the German bombers.

In Frederick Street, Flying Officer Ian Ritchie of 603 Squadron and his companions who had taken the afternoon off, heard the firing and dashed to their car. They broke every speed record on their way back to Turnhouse, but arrived too late to be sent up in their planes.

No one will ever know who fired the first shots in the aerial combats that followed. Pinkerton, after hearing that planes were bombing Rosyth, led his section north. He saw an enemy aircraft about three miles ahead of him flying east over a bank of cloud. He ordered his section into line astern to attack, and then McKellar drew his attention to three dark planes a little closer to hand, on the port side. Blue Section swung round to come down on their tail. Pinkerton was just about to fire when the planes turned to port and showed British markings. They were unfamiliar naval Sea Skuas, which none of the pilots had seen before. 'These chaps never knew how close they came to being shot down,' he says. The Skuas were training out of HMS *Merlin* from RNAS Donibristle. Later, 155 Brigade stated that their AA battery at Donibristle was hampered by Sea Skuas; presumably the same ones.

Pinkerton's section turned and chased after the first plane – except that by this time, Flying Officer Paul Webb had sheered off in some pursuit of his own. Climbing through a patch of cloud, Pinkerton saw the German through a small gap in the clouds some hundreds of feet below. 'Villa Blue Section, Tally Ho! . . . Buster,' announced Pinkerton. At that moment, Archie McKellar swooped down overhead to attack. The enemy was navigating along the north bank of the Forth, dodging in and out of the broken cloud. Each time he reappeared, McKellar or Pinkerton attacked.

Hauptmann Helmut Pohle in his Ju 88 was managing to duck most of the attacks. But eventually, to keep on course east, he was forced to leave the shelter of the cloud into the cloudless skies over the sea. He found McKellar on his port side and Pinkerton to starboard. Pohle climbed slightly and turned steeply to starboard, right into Pinkerton's guns at close range. That made Pohle dive fast to port; Pinkerton followed on his tail, firing the last few rounds of his ammunition. Pohle dived towards a merchant ship, flattened out at 500 feet, and then flopped on to the sea off May Island with grey wettish streams pouring out behind him, presumably petrol. Helmut Pohle's aircraft (Ju 88 – 4D + AK) was the second enemy aircraft to be shot down over Britain during the Second World War.

Helmut Pohle recalled:

'I was surprised by a Spitfire which I could not get away from. Also, we could not defend ourselves with the rear top gun, as this had gone with the canopy.'

You may recall that during his steep dive-attack on HMS *Southampton*, the top canopy of his Junkers had blown away.

'After another attack during which two of my crew were killed, one of the engines failed. Flying on with one engine I managed another 20 km, when – some distance off the Scottish coast – flying in an easterly direction, the next Spitfire attack destroyed the second engine too.

'Without both engines I must go down at sea. I saw a trawler, aimed to spring out near to the ship with my parachute, but the fourth man of my crew, the gunner of the rear below gun, was badly wounded. I was just able to clear the trawler before ditching the Junkers, although the sea was running at strength.'

Pinkerton and McKellar circled round at nought feet, and then Pinkerton flew back to the merchant ship, which had already altered course towards the sinking plane. Pinkerton flashed an SOS with his downward signalling lamp and waggled his wings; then he returned to the crash, and a moment later he and McKellar, their guns empty, hurried back to Drem to refuel and re-arm. The merchant ship rescued

Helmut Pohle who said: 'The crew of the trawler – I hoped it would be a Norwegian, then a neutral country – rescued me as well as my fourth crew member. However, I collapsed on the deck with concussion and face injuries. My crewman died from his injuries the next day.'

Afterwards Pohle was transferred to the destroyer HMS *Jervis*, where he was immediately interrogated by the ship's Paymaster Lieutenant Ralph Engledue, who spoke some German. The interrogation came to an end when Pohle lost consciousness again, due to the head injuries he had sustained.

The Crail Observer Corps post logged the crash at 2.55p.m. 602 Squadron had lost out to 603, as the first to shoot down a Nazi aircraft over Britain, by a mere ten minutes. Blue Section landed at Drem at 3.15p.m., but did not go up again until 3.54p.m. for another patrol.

The Observers at Crail were not the only people to witness the last few moments of *Hauptmann* Helmut Pohle's frantic attempts to evade the Spitfires of George Pinkerton and Archie McKellar. Peter Smith and his father, were on the Firth in their little fishing yawl. Mr Smith told me:

'There had been a north-easterly storm which in fact caused us to lose all of our lobster pots. The storm having abated, we were in our sailing yawl grappling for any pots that might have survived. It was a calm day, with plenty of sunshine over the sea, but some slow-moving cumulus clouds over the land. We would have been less than a mile off shore, about halfway between Anstruther and Pittenweem, on the north side of the Forth.

'Suddenly, from out of one of the clouds which seemed to stretch along the coast from Elic to Pittenweem, in a gap above us, there appeared a dark plane. It was obviously a German, and was being followed by two of our fighter aircraft. The Spitfires dived underneath him and peppered him with gunfire, before they seemed to disappear into the next cloud, which seemed to stretch all the way to Crail. Undoubtedly they had done the damage before they disappeared as the aircraft crashed into the sea just to the east of Fife Ness.'

The Forth Raid provides a vivid portrayal of the popular image of the auxiliary fighter pilot; glamorous, brave, adventurous, and a touch eccentric. What should never be overlooked is the importance of the auxiliary groundstaff, who operated in numerous trades, and who were the backbone of each squadron. After all, if there hadn't been airmen on the ground to re-arm and refuel the returning aircraft from each sortie, the battle could never have taken place.

As the fighter pilots of 602 Squadron returned to Drem that

afternoon, one of the groundcrew armourers was AC George Conway. George had joined the squadron in 1934 around the same time as Sandy Johnstone:

'He was a pilot officer and I was an aircraft member of groundstaff. 602 Squadron was a bomber squadron and therefore had a number of fully-trained air-gunners, of which I was one; until 1938 when the squadron converted to a fighter squadron. We were the first auxiliaries to receive Spitfires and the very first Spitfire I ever saw was flown into Abbotsinch by Squadron Leader Douglas Farquhar. The air-gunners were all only aircraft tradesmen with one corporal (Nobby Clark). I mention them, because although they had become temporarily redundant, in their own way they played a vital part in the battle on 16 October 1939. As well as myself, most other air-gunners remustered to armourer and we remained with our own flight and where possible re-armed our own pilots' guns after each sortie: on that day there were plenty of sorties.

'I was on holiday in Paris during August 1939 and whilst there I heard the wireless call from the UK telling all Britons to return home immediately. I returned home on 21 August and was called up two days later on the 23rd. My fiancé who was with me in France expected to meet me on the evening of the 23rd and was quite 'put about' when I was not available.

'The days leading up to the battle were spent cleaning guns, and practising re-arming until we were experts at it. During these exercises we discovered a method of arming a .303 Browning machine-gun which allowed the guns to have a bullet in the breech, and therefore gave the pilot a few extra seconds to get airborne and into action quickly. The arming of a Spitfire required one to kneel on the ground under the wing and lift up the quite heavy boxes of ammunition. We discovered that when the ground was wet – which it usually was – our knees got soaked through, so, we introduced leather knee caps. I had mine made by a blacksmith in Glasgow, who didn't charge me for them.

'The days were used profitably and when on 3 September war was declared, all personnel had to report for inoculation. The air raid sirens went off and we thought the war had really started. Two of the pilots had been recently married and they pitched tents in an adjoining field, which for a short time became their married quarters. I think the two pilots were Dunlop Urie and Finlay Boyd.

'A few days before 16 October 1939 an enemy aircraft had flown over us two or three times and on each occasion our pilots had been in the air but without finding anything. However, on the 16th the situation was different as the squadron was warned and ready for what occurred. Several "bandits" were seen and attacked. We heard gunfire and knew it was our own aircraft, being acquainted with the sound of eight .303 guns firing at the same time. It was only when they landed that we knew they had in fact been in combat, by the fabric gun port covers having been blown away. So we continued re-arming as necessary until the battle had finished.'

By this time three separate attacks had been made on ships of the Royal Navy anchored to the east of the Forth railway bridge, and as the time approached 3.00p.m., two of the German raiders had been shot down, but the day was far from over.

CHAPTER SEVEN

THOSE BLENHEIMS ARE GERMANS!

At Leuchars airfield to the north, 602's Green Section – Douglas Farquhar, Sandy Johnstone and Ian Ferguson – had just sat down in the Officers' Mess for a spot of lunch, while their Spitfires were being refuelled. Suddenly, the airfield's air raid sirens wailed and everybody in the Mess, except for Green Section, made hastily for the shelters. It was pointed out to the guest pilots that the station commander, Group Captain Brian Baker was all in favour of observing the proper form at such moments; and although the sirens were most likely just another practice exercise, it would be appreciated if they too moved towards the shelters provided. Sandy Johnstone who was still hungry, took the advantage of grabbing a bread roll from the table to take with him to their abrupt refuge. When Johnstone, Farquhar and Ferguson arrived at the nearest shelter, it was quite full. At no stretch of the imagination could the three of them squeeze into an already brimming crevice. They contemplated returning to the Mess to finish their lunch, but then decided that it would be bad manners to do so. Instead, as they couldn't actually get inside the shelter, they decided to scramble on top of it and sit down on the grass to await the all-clear. Johnstone was able to carry on munching his bread roll. For the next few minutes there was nothing to do except idly chat and watch a group of Blenheims move through the clouds towards Edinburgh.

Eventually Farquhar announced that he was going to find out what was going on. He slid down the side of the air raid shelter and disappeared inside the Mess from where he telephoned the Ops Room at Turnhouse. He discovered to his utter amazement that the Blenheims they had observed going towards Edinburgh, were in fact Germans! Unbeknown to Douglas Farquhar, Bob Johnstone at the Turnhouse Ops Room had received various direct orders from Air Vice-Marshal Richard Saul at No 13 Group Fighter Command Headquarters in

Newcastle, to 'Get up everything you can'. Aware of the fact that 602 Squadron had a flight on the ground at Leuchars, Richard Saul had insisted on their recall at 2.53p.m. Farquhar's subsequent telephone call to Turnhouse must have therefore come as tremendous relief to Bob Johnstone. Richard Saul was of course himself under enormous pressure to keep Fighter Command Headquarters at Bentley Priory updated on the progress of the battle. At 2.45p.m. he had been able to inform Air Chief Marshal Hugh Dowding, the Commander-in-Chief of Fighter Command, 'Had Tally Ho from four sections'.

Farquhar hurriedly informed his colleagues of the situation and before long a van was provided to take them back to their aircraft, refuelled and ready to go. In fact the three Spitfires had already been started. Farquhar and Ferguson strapped themselves in and took off immediately. Johnstone was a little less fortunate. Due to the fact that his aircraft had been the first one started, when he got there the engine temperature was off the clock, causing it to backfire and emit a cloud of black smoke as the throttle was opened. The few seconds as he coaxed the engine back must have seemed like an eternity, and when he did eventually get airborne, the other two Spitfires had become small specks somewhere in the distance. The time was a little after 3p.m.

Sandy Johnstone's troubles were far from over. A lone warrior he eventually arrived over the Forth, speeding towards the bridge. As he did so his aircraft began to rock with severe turbulence. He also noticed that all around him, puffs of a mysterious dark smoke kept appearing. The turbulence seemed to have a connection with the smoke. Looking down he soon realised that one of the ships below, in this instance the aircraft carrier HMS *Furious*, was firing everything they had at him with a vengeance. Not only could RAF fighter pilots mistake Ju 88s for Blenheims, Royal Navy guncrews could obviously mistake Spitfires for Ju 88s into the bargain. Johnstone remained alone and after shaking off the unwelcome attention of the Royal Navy he arrived over the Forth Bridge, where he could see no sign of friend or foe. Then suddenly, he spied a single raider in the distance climbing rapidly towards a bank of cloud to the east of Edinburgh. Hopelessly out of range he managed to fire off a short burst, before it disappeared out of sight. To this day he still isn't sure if it was a Blenheim or a Ju 88. Whatever it was, it managed to get away. And so ended Sandy Johnstone's – later to become Air Vice-Marshal Johnstone's – participation in that most historic of days.

The three German aircraft that had passed near Leuchars were the fourth and final wave of raiders. They had drifted north some considerable distance and were now heading south-west towards the target area. Among them was *Leutnant* Horst von Riesen.

Everything at this point became even more confusing: as well as aircraft flying east along the Firth of Forth, having already attacked the target area, there were now fresh aircraft flying in a south-westerly direction, towards the Forth Bridge.

As for those that had already perpetrated their attacks, Pohle and Storp were hugely unlucky. Helmut Pohle had deliberately and disadvantageously for himself remained over the target area, while the other two Ju 88s in his flight had effected their escape. Sigmund Storp seems to have attracted the attention of numerous Spitfires, while again, other members of his own flight and the flight which followed, made for home with little interference. However, at least a few of the other returning enemy aircraft were to be chased, although in rare exceptions with the concentration of fire power that had been brought to bear on the Ju 88 of Sigmund Storp. The enemy also became very scattered during their return journey, even more so than during their approach. Some had taken the most obvious return route, straight along the Firth of Forth. Others had hugged the north bank of the river, and others had flown low across the roof-tops of Edinburgh itself.

Eye-witness James Clark told me: 'On leaving the bridge area the planes had flown over Edinburgh itself at very low level. Many of the local populace thought it was a mock air raid. I am sure the steeple-jack who was repairing the tall chimney of Portobello Power Station at the time, didn't think it was funny when he had a burst of machine-gun fire sent at him. Luckily he was not injured. In a way it all finished as quietly as it had started, the RAF 602 and 603 Squadrons sorted Gerry out.'

I rather feel that the burst of machine-gun fire was intended more for the benefit of the gun emplacement that the Territorial Army had set up on top of Portobello Power Station, and which had opened fire on the enemy; rather than the unfortunate steeple-jack who happened to be in the wrong place at the wrong time.

At 2.40p.m. Chief Constable W. Morren in Edinburgh could clearly determine the sound of guns firing and shells bursting nearby. Looking out of his window he could see puffs of white smoke bursting through the air somewhere to the north-west. No air raid information had been received at the police station and at 2.45p.m. he telephoned the District Commissioner's office to see what was going on. No information was forthcoming as to the reason for the firing, and the District Commissioner's office in turn contacted the Regional Commissioner's office. At about 2.50p.m. Chief Constable Morren received a telephone call which informed him that an air raid had taken place on the Royal Navy warships at South Queensferry; but the raid was now over.

T. S. Johnston remembers the raid well, because like a lot of people, it was so unexpected that he just carried on with what he was doing as though nothing extraordinary was happening.

'The Germans caught everyone by surprise with this raid, and no air raid sirens sounded so people went about their daily tasks as normal. 'That is why I was with my mother in the gents and boys department of Leith Co-operative Store trying on new clothes that afternoon. The department was upstairs on the third floor some height above the ground. The salesman and my mother were in conference, while I stood, a bored eight-year-old: trying on clothes was not my favourite pastime. My boredom was, however, about to be broken with a sight that certainly did give me a thrill. The unmistakable drone of a German plane, it grew louder causing the glass in the window frame to vibrate. The three of us dived to the large window which faced north-west towards the bridge. Nothing to see at first and then into view swept an aircraft, travelling left to right across our vision. The German aeroplane was at roof-top height, probably 120–150 feet above the ground. He skipped over the roof-tops of the tenement flats of North Junction Street and flying east, disappeared from our view behind the Leith Hospital, which was on our right.

'The total time the plane was in view was probably only about ten seconds, but in that time I was able to make out the pilot's head in the cockpit. I think the plane was black or dark brown with the insignia of the Luftwaffe on the side and the swastika on the tail rudder.

'We all stood, astonished, because we were not aware that an enemy attack was in progress. Still at the window, surprised by what we had just seen, we heard another, higher pitched sound, which I now know to have been a Rolls-Royce Merlin engine, and into view came two Spitfires, flying the same course as the German aircraft. The heads of the pilots were clearly in view, and of course being up high we were almost at the same level as they were. The Spitfires crossed our field of vision much quicker than the German aeroplane had, and with a time gap of about twenty seconds between them, I have no doubt that they caught up with him.

'The course being taken when we saw them would have taken them over Leith Docks, out over the sea at Portobello Bay and back over land at Aberlady, but the German pilot may have altered course at any time. I don't know if this was one of the aircraft that was later shot down.'

In October 1939 Edinburgh Castle had been partly transformed into a military hospital, where Scottish soldiers were treated as they prepared to go to war. Most of the patients were undergoing very minor operations, or recovering from accidental injury caused during the rigours of their training. It was here that Pilot Officer G. Hunter of 603 Squadron, lay in a bed expecting a visit from the padre, Squadron Leader J. Rossie Brown. Little did he know that at that exact moment the padre was manning his machine-gun post at Turnhouse. For Pilot Officer Hunter, and the soldiers and airmen in the castle and the army nurses looking after them, it had been a very quiet morning; certainly no emergencies had been admitted.

The unusual sounds which were coming from outside, caused considerable excitement, drawing many of the patients to hang out the windows to get a better view of what was going on. All was well until the army nurse who was popping around the beds in the ward, noticed a severe draught, and ordered the gabbling soldiers back into their beds before somebody contracted pneumonia. The soldiers insisted that they could hear the sound of gunfire. The nurse went to the window herself, and looking out towards the Forth Bridge, could clearly see the flash of guns over the river. Eventually, the nurse returned order to the ward, but their excitement was far from over.

Margaret M. Pearson wrote her own account of the raid the day after it happened. Her story was sent to me via her son Mowbray, who lives in Edinburgh's Juniper Green. Before reading her vivid account, the following details will help to set the scene. At the time she lived in a country house on the outskirts of Edinburgh, a mile-and-a-half south of Edinburgh Airport – Turnhouse as it was then. Mowbray explains that they were a family of five children, but in October 1939 there was only the eldest sister, Mary aged 37, at home with her father and mother, aged 65 and 66 respectively.

In the narrative the first person to be mentioned was Jill. She was staying with her grandparents having been evacuated to what was considered by the authorities to be a 'safe place' in the country from Colinton, a suburb of Edinburgh. She was four and a half years old and 'Belinda' was her doll. She had her nanny with her. Mr and Mrs Wilson lived in the lodge with their deaf mute son George who helped about the place. The lodge where they lived was about 200 yards from the Pearsons' house. There the avenue met the public road, very close to the railway bridge mentioned later. John Proudfoot, always referred to in those days by his surname, was the full-time gardener. Mrs MacDonald was the cook. Billy was a wire-haired fox terrier. Ratho was the nearest village to the house and the name of the local policeman was Mr Cowe, to the roof of whose house the air raid siren had been affixed!

'It was a perfectly glorious afternoon and I sent Jill away at two to get ready for her walk. I was having my rest on the sofa and reading the paper. Dad and Mary went off to the garden to pick apples.

'I wanted to speak to Mrs Wilson about George and meant to go later, but I think it was just providence that made me look out at the window and think, "I must go out while the day is so gorgeous."

'When I was halfway down the avenue I came on Nannie with Jill wheeling her pram with Belinda in it. We walked down to the lodge together. I went in and spoke to Mrs Wilson and was then having last words before going up to speak to George, when the noise of very low-flying aeroplanes began. Mrs Wilson and I went round to the back of the lodge and then we heard screams and found Nannie leading back a terrified Jill. She came into the cottage and Mrs Wilson gave her some chocolate and we started off home. Jill clung round Nannie's neck and tried to cover her ears.

'At last I induced her to get into her pram by telling her we would get home sooner. She said at once, "Put up the hood." When the hood was up and the pram rattling over the stones we got on all right. Here was I raging and storming at the Air Force making such a noise over an evacuation area! There was no warning; so I did not think it was the real thing.

'We saw the maids standing at the railings near the back door of the house and I think bits of shell were rattling among the trees beside them. Some were supposed by Proudfoot to have fallen on the roof, but Dad went up and could not find any trace. Nannie and Jill both saw shells bursting in the sky before I joined them. They had only got about as far as the railway bridge as they were looking at things on the way.

'We got home and went to the nursery, but Jill was still worried, so I got her and Billy, who had been brought in from the garden as he was barking so much, down to the basement hall where Jill played ball with Billy and soon was laughing and they both thoroughly enjoyed themselves. Then I was able to go out and see what was doing. I met Proudfoot looking rather frightened, and then found Dad and Mary in the apple house. Mary had been up an apple tree when it all began, but it began to be a bit hot up there as things seemed to be falling; so she came down. Billy was with them and she said he rushed about barking at each explosion, but he was not frightened.

'Mary had come up to the house to look for me as they had left me on the sofa, but could find no one about except Mrs Macdonald calmly hanging out clothes at the back of the house.

'Mary thought she heard the warning after it was all over and I went out in the middle of tea to look at something and heard the Ratho "all clear" sounding. There is a siren now on the roof of Cowe's house.

'We had aeroplanes flying round us till about 6p.m. when they were all home. When Dad and I were standing outside the front door about 5p.m. a strong smell of gunpowder floated past us. Mary and Jill were feeding the hens and Jill noticed it too and asked what it was! The air was still and no wind; so I suppose it had taken some time to arrive here.

'Jill was rather jumpy about noises and aeroplanes all evening, but by this evening she seems all right again. She slept well and was not at all disturbed.'

CHAPTER EIGHT

BULLETS IN THE BEDROOM

The fishing yawl *Dayspring* which rescued Sigmund Storp, *Feldwebel* Hans Georg Hielscher and *Feldwebel* Hugo Rohnke, was skippered by Port Seton fisherman John Dickson; whose son, a crewman aboard the vessel said:

'We threw ropes to the crew of the sinking plane, and when we hauled them aboard we discovered that they were all wounded. They told us that another member of the crew had gone down with the plane. They were all young chaps.

'All three men were very grateful for being rescued, and the leader, who spoke English fairly well, took a gold signet ring from his finger and gave it to my father – the skipper. 'There's a ring for saving me,' he said.'

At first the crew of *Dayspring* had considered leaving the Germans to drown. This was not through malice, but in fear of what they might do once they came aboard. After all, they were fishermen, not soldiers, and it was quite possible that the Nazi airmen were armed and intending to hijack their vessel as an alternative mode of transport for their homeward passage.

As well as John Dickson's two sons William and John, Sandy and Andrew Harkness also crewed *Dayspring* that day on her voyage back from the May Island fishing grounds.

John Dickson, the skipper of *Dayspring*, said immediately he saw the aircraft ditch, which was approximately a mile away from the yawl when it hit the water, they went at full speed towards it. The aeroplane stayed on the surface for about five minutes and then disappeared below the waves. As the Junkers vanished, as well as his fears concerning the possible actions of the Nazi airmen, he wondered whether going to the rescue would serve any useful purpose. Surely, any survivors would have gone down with the aeroplane. Nevertheless, the crew decided to maintain their course and investigate the area, which at the time the Ju 88 submerged, was still a considerable distance away.

On arriving at the scene, three Germans were found clinging to an air-float. A rope was thrown out to them and one of the Germans, in sheer desperation, gripped it with his teeth, while the other two began to swim towards *Dayspring*. They were pulled aboard, shivering and exhausted. John Dickson said the Germans were given cigarettes and food, and warm, dry jumpers to put on. They didn't seem to be in the least bit hostile or aggressive, and showed their gratitude by vigourously shaking hands with all the boat's crew members. They appeared to consider themselves fortunate in being picked up alive. The skipper was informed that another member of the crew had gone down with the aeroplane, having been killed by machine-gun fire.

One of the Germans, undoubtedly Sigmund Storp, was said to be wearing an Iron Cross, when he was picked up.

None of the rescued Germans had been seriously injured, although each suffered from cuts, bruises, or bullet grazes; Hielscher perhaps the worst with a knock to his ribs.

Dayspring took her prized catch into Port Seton Harbour, where a crowd of local people was already beginning to gather. The three men were taken to the Police Station, where local GP Dr Black administered first aid. Hielscher was carried on a stretcher, as his injuries made it difficult for him to walk. On duty at the Police Station was Henry Stevenson, who was known as Harry during his Police service. His daughter Barbara Sibbald still lives in Edinburgh and remembers the day very well.

'He was the youngest son of a shepherd, born at a farm near Stenton, Dunbar, and spent his early years in East Lothian. He joined East Lothian Constabulary in 1924 and served in several stations until 1935 when he became "Station Man" at Cockenzie Police station which was situated in Port Seton. The Burgh was known as Cockenzie and Port Seton. His duties were that of the old-fashioned local bobby and included dealing with petty crime, domestic disputes, drunken brawls and visiting farms within his beat in connection with movement and diseases of animals. As I remember, he was well thought of by the locals and always willing to help them with their problems, a common one being helping someone get back into their house when they had locked themselves out. When my father was out my mother, Elspeth, answered the telephone and dealt with callers at the door.

'The outbreak of the war brought many changes which affected the whole family. The Police Station, a small office and two cells attached to our house, became temporary headquarters for the Local Defence Volunteers – the LDV which later became the Home Guard – and since the only telephone was situated in our front hall this meant a great deal of coming and going through our sitting room to make and receive telephone calls. The switch for the Air Raid Siren, situated on top of the local public house, was in the vestibule of our house and again if my father or the other Police Constable wasn't around, my mother switched on the warning and all-clear signals. The spare bedroom was fitted with racks to take protective clothing, respirators and rubber boots in readiness for a gas attack.

'On Monday 16 October, my father was too busy trying to balance his Fine Book – local people who had been fined at the Burgh Court paid their fines at the Station – and did not take too much notice of the air activity overhead. My sister Margaret, who was only four at the time, remembers being in the garden while my mother and Alec Craig, the young Police Constable, watched the planes overhead. By the time I arrived home from school, chaos reigned. I think the whole population of the Burgh had gathered at the Police Station as news had travelled fast that Germans had been brought in to the harbour on a fishing boat and were in the Police Station. There were no instructions in the Police Manual for dealing with this type of incident! Following telephone calls from my father, Sergeant Grant arrived from Prestonpans and Inspector Murray from Tranent – I presume they came by bus as there were no police vehicles attached to these stations. The Divisional Superintendent, M. Petrie also arrived from Haddington but he had a car at his disposal. I'm sure a great deal of discussion ensued. I know there was a lot of activity, so much so that our pet dog had to be tied to the table leg!

'Calls went out for dry clothing for the airmen, but one lady suggested a clothes rope might be more appropriate. The local publican sent a bottle of brandy round to the Police Station and I recall my father saying the airmen greatly appreciated that. Military Intelligence Officers arrived and the prisoners were taken by ambulance to Edinburgh Castle, taking with them our hot water bottles to help keep them warm and I can remember my mother reminding those in charge that the bottles were to be brought back. Alec Craig had provided some clothing for one of the airmen and when it was returned there was an Iron Cross in the jacket pocket. Although he was tempted to keep it, he thought it best to return it to the prisoner.

'On the evening of the 16th, Flight Lieutenant Gifford arrived at the Police Station to have a word about the day's events. My father and Alec were out, so while my mother made the visitor a cup of tea, Ines Craig (wife of Alec) and I went out to try and find them – no personal radios in those days!

'We duly located them and they returned to the office and talked over the day's events. I thought Flight Lieutenant Gifford was terribly handsome and from then on my ambition was to join the WAAF!

'It was indeed a very eventful and exciting day for us, so I would think it was one of the highlights of my father's police career. I know that my sister and I felt very proud of the fact that our father took charge of the first prisoners-of-war and at school I certainly basked in the reflected glory!'

Afterwards the three German prisoners were transferred to the military hospital in Edinburgh Castle. Although the sound of the battle going on outside had caused a great deal of excitement within the wards, as we read earlier, nobody suspected what was about to happen. Mid-afternoon, the ward sister told the nurses to make up three beds immediately. This in itself seemed peculiar to the nurses, as they had not been in the habit of dealing with emergencies; let alone German prisoners. Twenty minutes later half the population of Edinburgh seemed to converge on the castle. There were soldiers, airmen, fisher-men, policemen, stretcher-bearers, even the Lord Provost Sir Henry Steele, and the GOC of Scotland himself: who happened to be the Governor of Edinburgh Castle. Standing in the middle of all this were three bedraggled, extremely tired looking men, wearing what was by this time an odd assortment of borrowed clothes; including jumpers which the fishermen had given them after they had been rescued.

It was hardly a private affair and the other patients began to gather around the Germans excitedly, bombarding them with questions.

Eventually, as the fuss began to die down, the nurses began to skin the prisoners, in order to return the borrowed clothes, and get them into some dry pyjamas. Sigmund Storp, and his two companions, must have been tremendously relieved, when at last they were able to climb into warm, dry beds.

Oberleutnant Sigmund Storp and two of his crew members had been captured, and were now resting in the military hospital at Edinburgh Castle – another of his crew was dead. *Hauptmann* Helmut Pohle was onboard HMS *Jervis*, with two crew members dead and one mortally wounded. There were still ten Ju 88s and their crews unaccounted for.

Flight Lieutenant Marcus Robinson of 602 Squadron went after a plane at 6,000 feet over Musselburgh – and found a Spitfire of 603 Squadron on his own tail. Luckily the second pilot realised his mistake before any damage was done.

Edinburgh watchers saw Squadron Leader Douglas Farquhar, the commanding officer of 602 Squadron, tearing low across the city roof-tops chasing another German with his guns empty. Over his now working R/T he was yelling for more Spitfires to follow him.

Just before 4p.m. Flying Officer 'Bolster' Boulter of 603 Squadron, who had been patrolling with Flying Officers J. Cunningham, F. Rushmer, G. Wynne-Powell, and Pilot Officer B. Carbury, found a bomber over Inverkeithing and proceeded to give chase towards

Aberdour. The Ju 88 flew dangerously through the path of the anti-aircraft battery at RNAS Donibristle; followed, equally dangerously by Boulter's Spitfire. The AA shells burst furiously around the two aircraft – both emerged completely unscathed. The section's time up was 2.45p.m., they landed back at Turnhouse at 4p.m. precisely, although Wynne Powell had touched down first at 3.55p.m. Pilot Officer Charles Peel had taken off independently at 2.30p.m. and touched down at 3.20p.m., without success.

The most spectacular of all the pursuits was done at roof-height over Edinburgh and Portobello.

It started when Pilot Officer Colin (Robbie) Robertson of 603 Squadron, up on his second sortie of the afternoon, after re-arming at Turnhouse, found a bomber which had slipped inland and then turned for home. His time up on this sortie was 3.40p.m. 'Robbie' fastened on to the German who dived to nought feet to try and shake him off, and set off on a hedge-hopping run for home over Edinburgh. He passed straight over the airfield at Turnhouse at 300 feet at approximately 4p.m. The surprised gunners at the base didn't dare to open fire at the bomber in case they hit Robertson's Spitfire by mistake. The gun emplacements were of course fully manned, but ground interference was out of the question. As Robertson's Spitfire screamed overhead the guncrews – which of course included the padre, J. Rossie Brown – jumped up and down cheering ecstatically.

Pilot Officer Jim Morton who was still hoping to get another flight, didn't bother to wait for permission from Ops. On seeing the Ju 88 flash across the airfield hotly pursued by Colin Robertson, he rushed to his own Spitfire and set off in pursuit immediately. The Operations Record Book states his time up at 4p.m. He caught up with the two planes near Portobello and went straight into the attack. Two of his bullets drilled neat holes in the upstairs parlour window of the Lord Provost, Sir Henry Steele, and smashed the mirrored panel of an antique display cabinet, narrowly missing a priceless collection of ivories and china. However, one small Japanese vase was damaged. Sir Henry later found one of the bullets and formally returned it to 603 Squadron at Turnhouse.

Sir Henry's chauffeur, Alexander McMillan, said that at about four o'clock he heard the deep drone of planes, and on hearing gunfire, he warned the household. Then he went to the back door and heard bursts of gunfire. He saw one big machine and two of our own fighter machines close behind. Bullets seemed to be spraying down on the house.

Mr H. Robertson who lived in Portobello, explained how he found a bullet on a bed in his house. 'It crashed through the window, pierced the bedclothes, struck a bedside table, and finished up lying on a pillow.'

Another bullet struck a painter, Joseph McLuskie, on the side while he was painting the windows of a Portobello house. He was taken to Leith Hospital in a Police Ambulance, where he underwent an immediate operation to remove a bullet that had lodged near his stomach. A workman on some scaffolding fell off in his excitement as he craned to see the fight – but was unhurt. 'Man,' he said afterwards, 'a broken leg would ha'e been nothing jist to see yon sicht o' a lifetime.' John Ferry was hit in the leg at West Pilton as he worked on military installations, and was taken in a passing car to the Western General Hospital, where a bullet was extracted. At Davidson's Mains, bullets whizzed through the window of a house where Julia Hargreaves and her daughter Emma Riddel were showered by flying glass.

In the Royal Scots Club in Abercromby Place, a meeting was in progress. The Ju 88 screamed past the window, at which the chairman stopped in mid-address and exclaimed, 'My God, that's a Gerry!' A few moments later the expectant silence was again shattered by the pursuring Spitfires. After which the chairman continued with the meeting.

The German managed to shake off his attackers eventually with one engine damaged; and some time later, a plane supposedly came down in the sea off Northumberland.

Most of the Edinburgh citizens did not bother to take cover during all the activity. But there were hardly any casualties apart from Joseph McLuskie and John Ferry – and a dog that was mortally wounded in Alma Street, Inverkeithing.

While Flight Lieutenant Cairns Smith, the Flying Control Officer in the Drem Watch Hut, was desperately trying to get orders relayed in the general hubbub, Mrs Cairns Smith was out enjoying a quiet game of golf at Muirfield: quiet, that is to say, until a flurry of machine-gun fire overhead sent her scurrying into the nearest bunker (surely the first time that a golfer has gone willingly into a bunker!)

At least some of Edinburgh's gun batteries saw action that day. Some of these were manned by a local Territorial Army Regiment, the 94th City of Edinburgh Heavy Anti-Aircraft Regiment of the Royal Artillery. Not the best equipped of units, their ancient armoury could boast a 1917 Naval three-inch gun which was designed to shoot down aircraft moving at 100 mph; which was an acceptable velocity during the First World War. The unit could also muster a number of Lewis guns reminiscent, if not genuine artefacts from the first day of the Somme.

The roof-tops of Portobello became armoured installations; with the Ramsay Technical Institute and the Portobello Power Station donned by formidible batteries. The regiment was assigned the task of bringing down any German aircraft that presumed to approach the city from the

North Sea. Not surprisingly the expected targets for enemy incursions were the Rosyth Naval base and the Forth Rail Bridge.

When the guns were called to action on that fateful day, Major George Reid, who served with the 94th, later admitted that the regiment was very nervous about operating their First World War relics. They didn't know for certain that any of their weapons had been fired or examined since the end of the previous war. It was with some trepidation that the crews went into action; more terrified of their own guns exploding in their faces, than of being slain by enemy fire. Their anxieties were unnecessary as the batteries blasted out, albeit for a short baptismal, at the fleeing Germans.

Manning one of the Lewis gun sites was Jimmy Cranston with the Royal Army Ordnance Corps, who was in position at the Stirling Ordnance Depot RAOC in the Raploch District, beyond the western extent of the Forth. He recalls: 'The Argylls were firing from the castle, their target was a German who we assumed was apparently after the Forth Bridge and perhaps the ordnance depot itself. I am now 74 years old and therefore may not be 100% accurate, but I remember the 16 October well. Our CO that day was Major Ronald Crawford from the Royal Scots Regiment. I think he was related to the Crawford's biscuit people, but could be wrong. He was a Bisley Shot rifle expert, but also a real gentleman.'

Bearing in mind that the Germans attacked the ships three times initially, before they were intercepted, and then a fourth and final attack around 4p.m., individual aircraft may well have appeared at many points around the Firth of Forth, especially after the attacks had taken place. Mr Cranston's account which places them near Stirling, is the farthest point west that I am aware of. In my own mind, especially having heard the evidence of Sigmund Storp and Helmut Pohle, I doubt very much that any of the German aircraft did fly as far west as Stirling before the attack. As you will see later in the book, there was a lot of air activity over the Firth of Forth in the few days directly after the raid. It's quite possible that Mr Cranston has the date incorrect. Nevertheless, hard proof or not, as Mr Cranston's account only mentions the sighting of one enemy aircraft, there is always a possibility that when the bombers split up to avoid the Spitfires, one of them turned west towards Stirling, in a bid to escape before eventually turning east again for home.

James Sime was at school in Portobello.

'When the war started on 3 September I was eleven years of age and we were still on summer holiday from school and due to restart at the end of September.

109

'The opening of school was delayed for a couple of weeks as far as I recall and when we did start we did not attend the school but met in small groups in private houses. Our group met in a house near where I lived. There were about six in the group and one teacher, all from the school I attended, The Royal High School of Edinburgh. The group met for just a few hours in the morning, I think it was probably from about 10a.m. until noon. As far as I can recall on 16 October we were nearing the end of our stint at a house in Portobello, an easterly suburb of Edinburgh, when we heard gunfire and small puffs of cotton wool began to appear in the sky. The teacher thought it was an exercise as there had not been an air raid warning and he continued to teach. I should mention at this stage that we were being taught in a conservatory, a glass-house! At the appointed time we were released to go home, still with gunfire being heard. My route took me, by tramcar, past an electricity generating station at Portobello which was guarded by a Bofors anti-aircraft, gun on the nearby promenade. Just as we passed close to the gunsite it opened up and caused some alarm to the passengers on the train. Still there was no air raid warning – so it must be a practice!

'I arrived at my home about one-and-a-half miles away after a short time. There had been a lull in the firing and it was thought the exercise was over. However, shortly after I got indoors the noise of aircraft was heard. Being a bit of a plane spotter I stuck my head out of the window and was awarded with the sight of a German aeroplane passing over our house at about 150 feet being pursued by Spitfires of 602 or 603 Squadron of the AAF. When I said "That's a Gerry," I was ridiculed to some extent – "it can't be, there hasn't been a warning!" My father didn't say much – he had been in the First World War.'

While James Sime was attending school, albeit of a transitory nature, Francis Rennie who was twelve at the time, was playing truant. Standing in Stenhouse Drive with a friend, they watched with fascination as planes darted too and fro. They didn't for one moment realise the implications of what they saw, especially when a workman stopped next to them and very knowingly said, 'Aye – it must be a practice,' before he moved on down the street again.

Mr Angus McKenzie of Logie Green Gardens was only nine, and recollects:

'After the war was declared, my school was closed for a time, and as my mother and father were both working, I was looked after by my grandmother during the day, who lived in Bath Road, Leith, which was an entrance to Leith Docks and the River Forth. What I can remember quite clearly was playing in the street when I saw a plane, darkly camouflaged and wearing a black cross on the side of its fuselage. It seemed to be losing height and if my memory serves me right, smoke was coming out of it. The direction it was going was down the coast to Portobello. I thought it was going to crash. The rate of knots with which I ran up to my grannies house I think I would have won a gold medal.'

At the local Portobello picture house that day the film being screened was *The Adventures of Robin Hood* starring Errol Flynn and Olivia de Havilland. James Dick who was thirteen was in the auditorium with a pal. Coming out into the High Street late afternoon they were amazed to see a German aircraft 'house-high' being chased by two Spitfires. He could also hear and see two Lewis guns that had been placed on top of a flat roof in King's Road, firing up at the intruder.

Mr J. Hall-Livingstone remembers 16 October 1939 very well:

'I went to work as was usual that morning. I was serving my apprenticeship as an engineer in Edinburgh. There had been since the declaration of war in September a great deal of air activity in the skies over the capital. Spitfires of 603 and 602 were constantly whizzing overhead and quite low, which excited we apprentices no end. However, on this particular day we knew something special had happened as there was a more than usual aircraft presence over Edinburgh, also the crackle of machine-gun fire came over frequently.

'In those days 5.30p.m. was finishing time. I caught the 6.14p.m. train home to Portobello where I lived and all the talk in the carriage was of German raiders who had as was supposed then, tried to bomb the Forth Rail Bridge. On arrival at my home my mother told me that she watched a German plane from our house pursued by Spitfires fly low over Portobello. The local children had been collecting cartridge cases that had bounced from the roof-tops. Two of which adorned our mantelpiece for many years.'

Rita Darling was only seven at the time and had been evacuated to Kelty, a village between Dunfermline and Cowdenbeath on the northern side of the Forth.

'I had contracted scarlet fever and was in Dunfermline Fever Hospital. I had been allowed out in the grounds that day and a few other children and myself watched the dogfights, and there was the sound of machine-gun fire. It was all very exciting. A relative who was the designer in Dunfermline linen mills at that time, had a few table covers made with the air raid being the centre piece on them. I have kept the table cover which was a present to my mother.'

Mr Chris Prentice explained to me that the raid on the Firth of Forth was in fact his very first memory. He had always believed that the pilot was dead at that point.

'I was three and a half years old when the raid in October 1939 occurred. We stayed at what is now named Duddingston View in the Portobello area of the city. It was afternoon and I was playing with a little friend across the road, whose father was on sick leave following a nervous breakdown. Suddenly, we heard the drone of an aeroplane and we looked up to see this plane flying so low that we could actually see the pilot slumped in the cockpit; or at least his outline. In my child's mind I was sure that he was dead but you assured me that he lived.

'By this time my mother and other neighbours had gathered in the street and were horrified to see the German markings on the plane. My next memory of the plane is of it heading straight for the roof of a bungalow on the next street, forming a T with ours. By some miracle it rose enough to miss the house and flew on to eventually crash into the sea. The fact that the pilot was alive, as you have explained to me, perhaps accounts for what I always thought to have been a miracle. To us little boys it was all a great adventure but to the adults it must have been terrifying. My father later told me that the poor neighbour who was recovering from his nervous break-down, was in a dreadful state after this incident.'

Other pilots from 602 Squadron who saw action that day were Flight Lieutenant Dunlop Urie, who chased one of the raiders at just after 3p.m., all the way from the Forth Bridge to North Berwick, before it disappeared back across the North Sea. At 3.10p.m. Pilot Officer Norman Stone intercepted an intruder above Gullane which escaped his attentions, only to find itself being pursued by 603 Squadron. 603 and 602 seemed to be literally bumping into one another. Pilot Officer Hector MacLean almost came a cropper over May Island at about 3.30pm, when his own efforts to chase one of the intruders led him into a collision path with a 603 Spitfire. Luckily, the two aircraft missed each other by inches; however, the German had got away.

The Ju 88 that Dunlop Urie of 602 Squadron had intercepted over the Forth as he climbed out of his dive, was most probably one of the third wave of raiders. Dunlop Urie remembers the chase very well:

'About 1500 hours we (Yellow Section of A Flight) were ordered to patrol Rosyth. On our way there we saw a German Bomber climbing after he had obviously just dropped his bombs. We were about 3,000 feet and he would be about 5,000 feet. I gave a "Tally Ho" and put the Section into Line Astern.

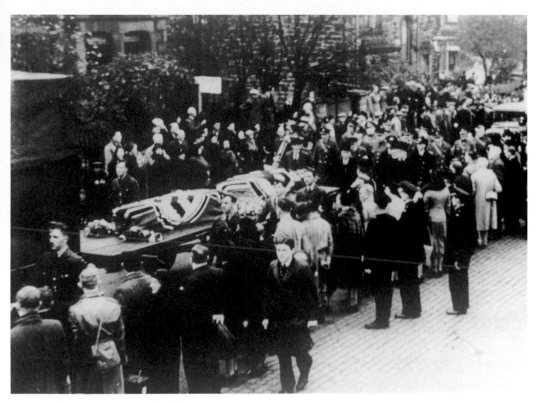

Draped in Swastika flags, and borne on trailers, the coffins of *Unteroffizier* Kurt Seydel and *Flieger* August Schleicher, move along Brunstane Road.
(Photograph courtesy of Andrew Jeffrey)

Buried with full military honours, *Unteroffizier* Kurt Seydel and *Flieger* August Schleicher, are laid to rest in Portobello Cemetery, 20 October 1939. A firing party of ten sounded a volley over their graves and pipers of 603 Squadron's pipe band played *Over the Sea to Skye*. *(Photograph courtesy of Andrew Jeffrey)*

The letter which George Pinkerton sent to Helmut Pohle on 22 October 1939. On the day after the raid, Pinkerton and Douglas Farquhar had visited Pohle in hospital. However, the meeting he refers to in the letter, was the one which took place in the sky over the Firth of Forth on the 16th: the other pilot mentioned was Archie McKellar. *(Photograph courtesy of Sir Hugh Dundas)*

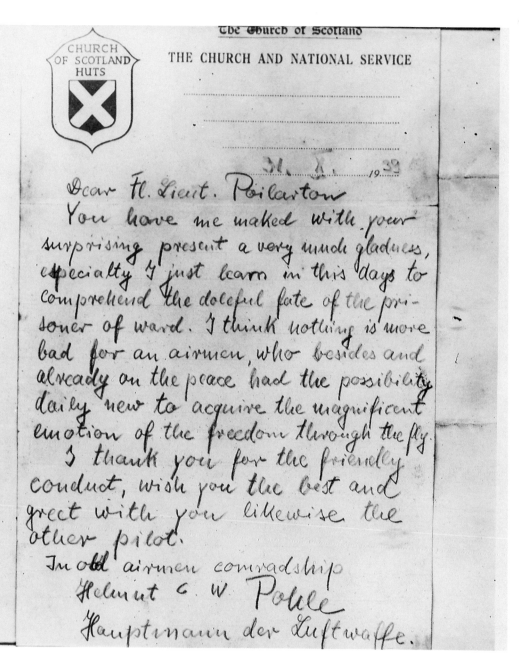

The letter from Helmut Pohle to George Pinkerton dated 31 October 1939, in which he thanks him for his present of sweets and cigarettes.

(Photograph courtesy of Sir Hugh Dundas)

A postcard which was produced by Caithness Bros, Kirkcaldy, which gives an artist's account of the first Nazi raid over Scotland. The dramatic scene which shows the two German aircraft about to crash below the Forth Bridge, is of course, inaccurate. The two aircraft were brought down off Port Seton and Crail respectively.
(Photograph courtesy of J. Montgomery)

The badge of 603 (City of Edinburgh Squadron) Auxiliary Air Force. As a Bomber Squadron the unit's badge embodied a three-turreted castle, closely resembling the crest of the City of Edinburgh, and designed to emphasise the close relationship between the City and the Squadron. Surmounting the central feature was the representation of an eagle with outstretched wings symbolic of flight. Following consultation with the civic authorities, the Lord Lyon King of Arms and the Chester Herald of Arms in London, a new badge was evolved and officially approved. Note the letter (F) denoting Fighter Squadron. *(Photograph courtesy of George Mullay)*

I set the gun-sights for a Heinkel at 400 yards. It had been constantly drummed into us that we must not get closer than that and the guns were trained to give maximum striking power at that range. The enemy aircraft had obviously not seen us and I was able to get him very exactly in my sight, and his wing tips coincided with the 400 yard mark. I opened fire and saw my bullets hit him. This was the first time I had fired a Spitfire's guns and much to my surprise, my nose dropped with the recoil. I corrected this but as I did so the enemy aircraft started to dive very steeply. I followed him down and gave him another burst then broke to allow my No 2 and No 3 to have a go. By this time he would be about 50 feet above the sea flying east off North Berwick. I had another go at him but always keeping 400 yards from him. One of his engines had stopped and my No's 2 and 3, each had another go. He continued to fly over the sea and parallel to the coast and although we had exhausted our ammunition we continued to follow him. Two Spitfires of 603 Squadron joined us and also had a go. When he reached St Abb's Head he was still flying on one engine and I decided there was no more we could do. He had been shot at by five fighters and I would be very surprised if he would cross the North Sea. Undoubtedly if we had closed to 200 yards he would have been destroyed. This is hindsight. Our orders were very clear and given many times over.'

Dunlop Urie had intercepted his raider as he approached the Forth Bridge just after 3p.m., by which time the air raid over Rosyth had lasted for a good half hour. At this point there was a lull in the action over the target area itself. Little damage had been done by any of these first nine aircraft, and few injuries sustained. The Royal Navy, in the apparent aftermath of the attack, began to investigate the damage, totally unaware that the Luftwaffe had one more surprise in store.

CHAPTER NINE

ACTION STATIONS

A convoy of British and neutral vessels had been making its way south from Scapa Flow during the previous night. Simultaneously, another convoy had been sailing north from Gibraltar. Meanwhile, some of the cruisers from Vice-Admiral Sir Edward Collins 2nd Cruiser Squadron had been on a sweep towards the coast of Norway. By the morning of the 16th, the cruisers, along with the destroyers *Jersey, Janus* and *Jackal*, had become part of the escort. HMS *Mohawk* and HMS *Jervis* had joined the convoy during the morning of the 16th, and the cruisers, escorted by *Jersey, Janus* and *Jackal*, left at high speed for their moorings next to the Forth bridge. This left just the *Mohawk* and *Jervis* to shepherd the convoy up-river.

It was 3.20p.m. and HMS *Mohawk* was sailing down the Firth of Forth from the North Sea and was passing between Kincraig Point on the north shore, and Gullane on the south; some twenty-five miles out of Rosyth. There were hardly any clouds over the water and visibility was excellent.

On 16 October 1939 John Kerr was a Royal Navy gunner aboard HMS *Mohawk*. HMS *Mohawk* was a destroyer of the Tribal class, authorised in the 1935 Naval programme. She was built by John I. Thornycroft and Co. Ltd, at Woolston, Southampton, and was laid down on 16 July 1936. She was launched on 8 June 1937; and completed on 10 June 1938. The *Mohawk* joined the 4th Destroyer Flotilla, which was with the Mediterranean Fleet when the Second World War broke out on 3 September 1939. This flotilla returned home in October 1939, allocated to the Rosyth Command.

John Kerr who now lives in Dalkeith explains:

'We had been in the Mediterranean Sea since February 1938. We were ordered to proceed to Aden and while we were going through the Red Sea, war was declared. We were immediately ordered back to Gibraltar, to pick up a Scandinavian convoy that would take us back to the Forth.

'As we entered the Firth of Forth I had just come off watch. It was piped over the tannoy that we would arrive in Rosyth at 1600. There was going to be a long-deserved shore leave. I was going to surprise my family so I went to get a shower before going ashore. At this point the Rattlers went to action stations. We thought it was just an exercise, so I dropped everything and put on my boiler suit. I ran to my action station which was "A" Gun on the fo'csle, a 4.7-gun (Twin). I arrived there with Petty Officer Buffer. We saw something like a barrel land in the water right next to the ship. It exploded and both Petty Officer Buffer and I fell to the ground wounded by flying shrapnel. The next thing I knew I was being picked up off the deck with a bit of shrapnel sticking out of my head. One minute we were all laughing and joking; the next many were dead and injured. So much for the alertness of those whose job it was to be on the look-out for raiders. The first warning we got was the rattle of guns.'

The German bombs which burst on the water near the *Mohawk* and the accompanying machine-gun fire, caused a total of twenty-five casualties. Her captain, Commander R.F. Jolly was fatally wounded in the stomach. Refusing medical attention, he remained on the bridge and continued to direct the ship's passage home. He died five hours later and was posthumously awarded the Empire Gallantry Medal. The explosion that fatally wounded the captain, also claimed the lives of Lieutenant E.J. O'Shea and fourteen other members of the ship's company; a total of sixteen officers and other ranks. John Kerr remembers a few of his friends and colleagues:

'CPO Dent, Sick Bay Artificer; Seamen Mason; Seaman Richardson; two boys who had just been made up to Ordinary Seamen, called Roebuck and Traynor; Petty Officer Coward, Seaman Whatley and Seamen Hatchen.'

Commander Jolly was detested by the men who served under him. John Kerr goes on to describe something of the *Mohawk's* captain who died so gallantly that day.

'He had seven pairs of white gloves. A pair for each day of the week. Every Saturday we had Captain's Inspection, and the ship had to be scrubbed and polished. He would come around just before dinner and pass his hand over all the pipes etc. If his white gloves happened to get a wee bit dirty, everything had to be redone. He would go no further until it was reported to him, that the ship was ready for further inspection. As this always happened on a Saturday we had the impression that he did this deliberately to keep us onboard, because on a Saturday or Sunday we could go ashore earlier than usual.

'I can recall once my mate was QM (Quarter Master) at the Quarter deck in Malta Grand Harbour, which was always heaving with our ships (when we had a Navy). One of the destroyers was leaving harbour and started hooting. When Commander Jolly came up from the wardroom and asked which ship was leaving, my mate gave him the number on the ship's side. Because he didn't know the name of the ship, Jolly put him on a charge and he got three days' leave taken away and pay punishment. He was not a nice skipper and no-one liked him. In fact, if I was walking up the deck and I saw him coming from aft, I used to cross over from starboard to port side to avoid him.

'I joined the ship in 1938 when we were in the Med Fleet. Commander Jolly had come from the aircraft carrier HMS *Hermes*. His period with the *Hermes* was known as the "White Lady", because of his strict cleaning routines. Mind you, our ship HMS *Mohawk* was never dirty.

'Our skipper after Commander Jolly was called Commander Eaton, and what a man he was. We would have gone from here to hell with him. He was a man's man and he was great in action. I think he died only about five or six years ago. God look after him wherever he is. When we were sunk on 13 April 1941 off Cape Bon, we had to literally force him into the water.'

Lieutenant O'Shea who was also killed during the Forth Raid, was not popular with the *Mohawk*'s crew either. A 'square-jawed Irish man', who according to John Kerr 'had risen from the ranks'.

The attack on HMS *Mohawk* had taken place at 3.25p.m., half an hour after the main raid on Rosyth. The aircraft that had attacked the *Mohawk* was one of the three raiders from the final wave, who had somehow drifted so far north that they had been visible from Leuchars by Douglas Farquhar and Sandy Johnstone. They had flown south-west towards the north coast of the Firth of Forth, where a convoy had been observed. Their brief was to attack naval targets. Only one of these aircraft had made the attack on the *Mohawk*, while the other two aircraft in the flight had continued on their set course to Rosyth. The other two aircraft were the final raiders to be seen over the prescribed target area, and one of these was the Ju 88 that Pilot Officer Colin 'Robbie' Robertson and Pilot Officer Jim 'Black' Morton had chased over the roof-tops of Edinburgh. This aircraft had flown directly over Turnhouse itself at 4p.m.

Several people had seen the attack on the *Mohawk*, and perhaps the best view would have been afforded to the fishermen who were operating their yawls that day around the Isle of May.

Peter Smith, who had already witnessed the shooting down of Helmut Pohle from his fishing yawl told me:

'I noticed a small convoy of ships coming from the north, approaching the Isle of May. The destroyer which accompanied the convoy started to behave in a very odd manner, darting about at great speed. I mentioned it to my father who suggested that there might have been a submarine about: he was more interested in getting on with his work.

'A little while later another destroyer appeared heading west, just off Elie Ness. We later discovered it was the *Mohawk*. Suddenly I saw a dark plane appear in the sky, which seemed to be heading straight towards the *Mohawk* from the north-east. I didn't hear any guns from the *Mohawk* before the bomb was dropped. I thought the destroyer had been sunk as the spray completely hid her. Then all the guns opened up as the plane turned south.

'Many people saw this incident and I talked to a chap who was on top of the local town hall, working with his father as a plumber and he said the *Mohawk*'s stern jumped out of the water, with the near miss of the bomb. I assume that the *Mohawk* was caught unawares, and alas the German aircraft appeared to escape from its fire.'

The Luftwaffe, quite unintentionally, had kept their worst surprise to the end. Unintentional because their main target was HMS *Hood* (*Repulse*) which had been observed that morning entering the Firth of Forth from the North Sea. If the *Hood* was in dry dock their secondary targets would be any other Royal Navy vessels, anchored at Rosyth. The German pilot who attacked the *Mohawk* could not have known before-hand that a convoy, accompanied by a destroyer was heading down river, unless they had received a message from one of the other Ju 88s that had already flown over Rosyth, which informed him that the *Hood* was already in dock, and therefore out of their reach, and that other ships had been observed sailing up the Forth from May Island. Of course this is only supposition many years later, but you cannot help but wonder why the pilot broke away from his formation and never arrived over the intended target, with the other two aircraft in his flight.

Other than the recollections of Helmut Pohle and Sigmund Storp, there is little to go on to get the German point of view. One of the other pilots of the first *Gruppe* of *Kampfgeschwader* 30 (1 KG 30), who had flown during the raid was a young *Leutnant* – later promoted to Colonel – named Horst von Riesen. Through von Riesen's own account written long after the war, Dunlop Urie feels confident that this was the young German he had chased.

Arriving over the target, probably with the third wave of Ju 88s, von Riesen had also discovered that the *Hood* was in dock. Just to the east of the Forth Railway Bridge he noticed the cruisers and took one into his sights. He scored a near miss. As he began to climb away from his dive-attack, his radio operator observed that several fighter aircraft were descending on them. Von Riesen knew instinctively that he was going to need all the speed he could squeeze out of his Junkers. He pushed down the nose, and dived for the sea, throttle wide open. It was hopeless! The Spitfires had the advantage of speed and height from the start and they had soon caught him up. Low over the Forth, von Riesen could quite clearly see the splashes from the shells of the shore batteries, as they began to join in the attack against him. He thought he was finished. Guns were firing at him from all sides, and the Spitfires behind seemed to be taking turns at attacking. However, his Ju 88 was continually gaining speed, until he was doing 250 mph. The Junkers' speed must have been quite a surprise to the Spitfire pilots. Von Riesen also jinked from side to side, to impede the accuracy of their guns. He saw what appeared to him to be raindrops splashing on the surface of the water. These were the bullets from the guns of the Auxiliary Air Force.

His two allies were time and fuel. He carried far more fuel than the Spitfires, and every minute he was able to keep going, meant he was a further seven kilometres closer to Westerland, and the Spitfires were a further seven kilometres away from their own bases. Reaching the open sea, he knew that eventually the Spitfires would run low on fuel and be forced to give up the chase.

All seemed to be going well until inevitably bullets began to hit their target and white smoke was observed to be belching out of one of his Ju's Jumo engines. Bullets had pierced the radiator releasing its coolant, without which the motor was finished. Von Riesen was forced into switching it down before it burst into flames.

He was now flying only a few metres above the water. His speed had sagged to 112 mph. All he could do now was wait for the kill. However, after travelling several miles out across the North Sea, von Riesen was surprised to discover that his pursuers had turned back.

Heading home, took all the pilot's strength to hold the Ju 88 straight against the violent torque of the second engine. He was barely managing to keep the craft clear of the waves. He had a difficult decision to make; either to limp the four hundred miles back to Westerland; or to turn back to Scotland. He had doubts about whether the aircraft would be able to maintain its height on just one engine, but his crew unanimously detested the thought of returning to face the Spitfires. They opted to take their chance against the sea, with a risk of drowning or dying from exposure, rather than return to face the Spitfires.

As the flight continued and the fuel burned, the aircraft became lighter, and von Riesen was able to coax it a little higher.

Four hours later the crippled Ju 88, flown by *Leutnant* Horst von

Riesen, and his exhausted crew, limped back into their base at Westerland. In dribs and drabs the other aeroplanes began to reappear out of the dark October sky. Horst von Riesen had survived against Spitfires; he would meet them again during the Battle of Britain, over the Mediterranean and during the Battle for Sicily.

The final reports from the Observer Corps Area Centre at Galashiels, stated that at 4.20p.m. an Observer was sent from A2 Post at Athelstaneford near Haddington to investigate an aircraft which was believed to have landed. At 4.40p.m. A2 Post reported that the aircraft had risen again, and was seen to be flying eastwards; it had now been joined by a second enemy aircraft. I doubt that either of these aircraft had actually landed, they were merely flying extremely low, hedge-hopping, in order to avoid the attention of the Spitfires. At 4.55p.m. A2 Post reported that a two-engined bomber, followed by another bomber, came low behind a screen of trees, skimmed the ground and flew out to sea. This was the last confirmed sighting of any of the Forth Raiders over Great Britain. At 5.10p.m. the Observer Corps Centre at Galashiels passed all of its information to Turnhouse; at 5.15p.m. all records were sent to Observer Corps Headquarters in Edinburgh.

There has never been any real confirmation of the number of enemy aircraft brought down that day. Pohle and Storp made two; a third was believed to come down near the Northumberland coast; and even a fourth was claimed by some to have been unable to make it home. One, or indeed both of these last two aircraft, could well have been that of *Leutnant* Horst von Riesen, whom we know for a fact, did reach home.

So many eye-witnesses gave thrilling accounts of German aircraft being shot down by the drove, either by our own fighters or by the anti-aircraft batteries, that if each story was believed to be true, the number of enemy planes shot down could well have exceeded the planes that were actually operating over Scotland that day. As far as I am concerned, the only hard evidence available suggests that the two Ju 88s flown by Sigmund Storp and Helmut Pohle were the only casualties of the day.

On the following afternoon a large crowd of excited people gathered at Port Seton harbour. The news had spread that two local fishing boats – the *East Lothian* and the *Andrina Falconer* – were towing in one of the crashed German bombers. It transpired however, that the boats were towing only a wheel and part of the undercarriage of the Ju 88. These were examined by RAF officers and taken away in the back of a truck.

CHAPTER TEN

SHOOTING A LINE

The fighter pilots of 602 and 603 Squadrons who had gone up thinking this was all 'just another flap' came down tremendously exhilarated. Airmen rushed to their planes the moment they landed to hear the latest news. Intelligence officers rushed about trying to piece together a coherent story, almost standing on their heads with excitement.

Most excited of all, perhaps, were the two bull terriers who lived at Drem with 602 Squadron – the pure-white Miss Villa Voop (Villa was the signals name for 602) and her brother Marco, who was white with one black eye. Exotic Villa Voop, who drank tea and had a bath every night with her owner Flying Officer Muspratt Williams in scented rose-water, and the more spartanly reared Marco (owned by Flying Officer Donald 'Duck' Jack), went tearing about barking their heads off with glee.

By tea-time it was all over. Storp and Pohle had been fished out of the North Sea. The Scottish pilots had got together and agreed that it had been a very pleasant, if rather chaotic, joy-ride. They realised that the bullet groupings on their Spitfires (a 27-foot spread at 400 yards range) was too ineffectual to hurt the Germans, and started drawing hundreds of little circles on pieces of paper to prove their point.

Outside the airfields the rumours were beginning to fly. Eye-witnesses up and down the east coast of Scotland claimed to have seen planes crashing in flames by the droves.

Pinkerton had a cup of tea with his section, and at 3.54p.m. his section was ordered up to patrol the Forth Bridge at Angels Fourteen. There were hopes that a second wave of bombers were on their way, but the last of the flap was over. 602 and 603 had been blooded, and scored the first success against the professional pilots of the Luftwaffe. They never managed to have a big party to celebrate, that night, both flights of both sections were on duty again. Total damage to the squadrons – two bullet holes (Gilroy's and McKellar's planes).

To this day Patsy Gifford, George Pinkerton and Archie McKellar

120

have been attributed to the slaying of the first Nazi dragons. As I think this account in some part suggests, the whole shooting match was something of a free-for-all. One, two, three, four Spitfires and more attacking the same enemy aircraft. There were those who felt that the three above-mentioned pilots should not have been given all the credit.

Jim Morton wrote in his diary about 16 October 1939.

'Very nice day. Cloud 2-3/10 cumulus 3,000. Slight ground haze. No wind. 1425: "A" Flight ordered off. Red Section – P. Gifford, Ken Macdonald, Colin Robertson, to patrol Drem. Yellow Section – George Denholm, "Sheep" Gilroy and self likewise. Took off 3 minutes after Red Section. At 2,000 feet to the west of the airfield saw 4 ack-ack bursts in line 400 yd to the right of us. Almost immediately saw 3 or 4 enemy aircraft circling over the Forth Bridge at about 5,000 feet. Informed George, but he had already spotted 3 aircraft to the south of us at 3,000 ft. pursuing these in line astern. Enemy making for a bank of cloud over Currie. Followed "Sheep" through a gap in the cloud, George in the lead, firing at one of the enemy. At the other side of the cloud there was no sign of George. "Sheep" was pursuing one turning away to port.

'I took the starboard machine and followed it through two more clouds shooting short bursts from a low No 1 position. Enemy speed 160-180 mph. Enemy fired tracer apparently from two guns. He turned east in the third cloud, and near Dalkeith I got in a burst of about eight seconds from a high No 1 position. Enemy failed to make the next cloud and started to lose height swinging north to Wallyford. At the end of this long burst, a large black piece fell off the enemy port wing and port engine slowed down. Was about to make a further attack when Red Section shot past me from above. I called out to "Patsy", but there was no reply, and as they had obviously not seen me and I was almost out of ammunition, broke away and returned to re-arm. The last I saw of the enemy was at 500 feet over Prestonpans being vigorously attacked by Red Section. He eventually came down in the sea off Port Seton – one dead – three prisoners. Gifford considers this his trophy, but prisoners and Robertson confirm he was disabled (port engine U/S) before Red Section appeared. Whether this was due to my fire or to previous fire from George Denholm is unknown. I certainly hit him because return fire stopped during my second attack.'

Jim 'Black' Morton was badly burnt when shot down on 5 October 1940. He subsequently flew Beaufighters and won a bar to his DFC. He died about eight or nine years ago. His account bears similarities to both Storp's and Gifford's. Storp said: 'My gunner had been killed in the first burst.' Gifford admitted himself that before the final kill: 'The rear-gunner was silent. As soon as the Spitfire in front of me had broken away after giving him another burst, I went close in and gave him all I had.' Presumably the other Spitfire he refers to was Jim Morton.

Jim Morton's account paints an extremely graphic picture of those first crucial moments above the target area. According to him, at the time the section got airborne, they could already see the first three raiders (Pohle) over the Forth Bridge, while to the south, they observed another three aircraft (Storp) approaching. As with all accounts, there are a number of contradictions in the detail, the most startling being the height at which he put the raiders. You may recall that Pohle was first observed over the target area by the AA battery at Dalmeny Park, who estimated his height at 10,000 feet. Helmut Pohle said himself that his dive-attack had taken place from 12,000 feet to 1,800 feet. Pohle's account could be misconstrued, and he could well mean that he was flying at 12,000 feet during his approach to the target. Morton on the other hand puts their height over the bridge as 5,000 feet. I suspect the actual height from which the dive took place was somewhere between the two.

Morton also wrote in his diary an account of the second sortie, when he chased one of the last two raiders over the rooftops of Edinburgh just after 4p.m.

'1610: One enemy approached the aerodrome from the west at less than 50 feet with two Spitfires in attendance. Took off independently in great haste – with cockpit door open. Had to make a steep turn at 0 feet and 100 mph to avoid a Moth taking off at the same time. Enemy carried on over Edinburgh and turned to follow the coast. By taking a short cut, caught up with him at Portobello Power Station. Opened fire from 500 yards on starboard quarter in order to put him off in case he was about to bomb the power station. Fired all ammunition in two long bursts for most of the first burst was misled by the tracers and used them instead of sight. Most seemed to pass just in front of his nose. Second burst from astern was much better, enemy swung inland over Newhailes and then east again over Musselburgh. Enemy speed 140-160 mph at 200 to 300 feet. There was no return fire. There was another Spitfire in attendance, so when I had finished my ammunition returned for more. The other Spitfire turned out to be Robertson who had followed the enemy from up the Forth and reckoned he had killed the air-gunner. Enemy crossed the coast at 140 mph and disappeared out to sea at 0 feet. Very disappointing result. He should have come down. Very luckily there seem to be no civilian casualties in Portobello, the only damage being to some furniture in the Lord Provost's house which looks as if it could do with it. Later reports say there was another enemy went away like this on one engine after being shot at by 602.'

The following report is taken from 603 Squadron's Operations Record Book, written on the day of the raid itself, and it is of interest to note that as the raid was taking place, the enemy aircraft were always referred to as Heinkels.

'Red Section shot down 1 enemy aircraft (thought to be a Heinkel 111) east of Dalkeith. Aircraft fell into sea off Port Seton. Enemy aircraft believed to be one of the three intercepted by Yellow Section. 3 prisoners were rescued from the crew of 4.

'Yellow Section intercepted 3 enemy aircraft over Dalkeith and despite the fact that the enemy aircraft broke formation and took advantage of clouds, rounds were fired at each one of them. L.1048 received 1 bullet through the top engine cover. Damage to enemy not known.'

Hauptmann Helmut Pohle and his seriously wounded fourth crewman were taken to Port Edgar Hospital near South Queensferry. He remembered nothing of his short interrogation by the Paymaster onboard HMS *Jervis*. 'Some time later I regained consciousness,' he said; 'a white bed and a nurse. I thought that I was in Norway. However, I was in the Royal Navy Hospital at Port Edgar, near Edinburgh. At the head of my bed stood an RAF Intelligence Officer. About ten days later I was transferred to a military hospital in Edinburgh Castle.'

John Kerr, the Royal Navy gunner who was wounded when the massive explosion rocked the *Mohawk*, which caused all the Navy's fatalities that day, was also taken to Port Edgar Hospital; along with PO Buffer who was wounded beside him at their action station.

According to John Kerr, Pohle seemed nervous about how he was going to be treated by the British. After all, he was one of the first Luftwaffe men to find himself in such a precarious position. There was no way of knowing the fate that awaited him. Unlike Sigmund Storp, who was already at Edinburgh Castle, he was completely on his own. Perhaps his nervousness was enhanced by an inward sense of guilt and shame for the barbarous act he had recently perpetrated.

John Kerr explains: 'I was taken into a ward after I had been attended too. The next day the German was put in the same ward. All the time he acted as if someone was going to give him a pill, he even hesitated before drinking a cup of tea.'

The next day, George Pinkerton went with Squadron Leader Douglas Farquhar to Port Edgar Hospital to visit Helmut Pohle, the German which he had shot down. Pohle was bandaged to the eyes – he had smacked his face against his instrument panel when his plane ditched. Says Pinkerton, 'He was very nice, a bit German officer-ish. He told us that he had had very strict instructions not to bomb the bridge or any land targets. Later I sent him sweets and cigarettes and wrote to him. I got a very nice letter back.'

Pinkerton's letter, which was dated 22 October 1939 and addressed to the Air Ministry, London, read as follows:

'Dear *Hauptmann* Pohle, I much appreciated the opportunity of meeting you on Monday last, and I hope you are now feeling more comfortable and on the way to a speedy recovery from your injuries. We are at war, but that fact does not prevent me from acknowledging the very gallant fight which you put up. These sweets and cigarettes which I ask you to accept, are an evidence of my good wishes to you and of my hope that in due course you will have a happy reunion with your people at home. The other pilot who was with me when you came down wishes to be associated with me in this expression of goodwill. With my deepest respects, G.C.P.'

Pohle's reply, written on 31 October 1939, upon The Church of Scotland headed paper, reads: (and I have left the spelling exactly as he wrote it):

'Dear Fl. Lieut. Poilarton, You have me maked with your surprising present a very much gladness, especialty I just learn in this days to comprehend the doleful fate of the prisoner of ward. I think nothing is more bad for an airman, who besides and already on the peace had the possibility daily new to acquire the magnificent emotion of the freedom through the fly. I thank you for the friendly conduct, wish you the best and greet with you likewise the other pilot. In old airmen comradship, Helmut C.W. Pohle *Hauptmann der Luftwaffe.*'

Pohle remembered the day he was taken to the Military Hospital at Edinburgh Castle. He wrote this account in 1987, and as you can see his English had improved somewhat over the intervening years.

'One of the last days of October 1939 I was transported on a stretcher from Port Edgar to the War Hospital. I remember it was a little one-bedroom. A kind of tower room with a little window in a niche. On the side of my bed stood an arm-chair.'

Pohle explained that a British soldier always sat in the chair, relieved every four hours.

'Most of them slept after a time of thirty minutes and consumption of a few cigarettes – the rifle between their knees. Many times the rifle fell down to the floor with a crash. Nevertheless I could see with one eye – the other was blindfolded because of some cuts – the rifles were saved every time and the poor boys out of danger.'

During his few weeks at the hospital Pohle thought he received excellent medical attention. 'Every day came the chief medical officer. Good morning, how are you feeling?' He explained how he was visited by an ophthalmic surgeon who tested his eye, and a dental surgeon. 'Three of my lower jaw front teeth were declined forwards after the crash at sea.' Apparently the dental surgeon fitted him with a clamp which he turned tighter every second day. Pohle had little confidence in such dentistry but after six days his teeth were back in their correct position. Forty-six years later he admitted that they were still in the same position. Pohle said the surgeons were not military, but civilians from the city. Pohle's recovery was a slow process, but in time he was able to get out of bed and look at the view of Edinburgh from his tiny window, from where he could see 'a business street with many trade houses'.

During the last week in November he was allowed to take a walk around the castle. He was accompanied by one of his rifle-toting guards, who helped explain all the objects of interest, and was apparently very knowledgeable regarding the castle and Edinburgh in general. 'For this walk I get a kind of jogging suit; a sky-blue blouse, white trousers and a red band.' Pohle didn't know what to do with the red band, but it was explained that Queen Victoria herself had introduced this particular suit to be worn by sick British soldiers: the red band was to be worn around the neck.

On one of his last days at the hospital he was taken into a large ward filled with British soldiers, where a choir of young ladies were giving a concert, dressed as fishwives. They even had large plastic fish, which they frequently struck against their thighs, to the exuberant applause of the British patients. You must admit, Pohle was certainly getting an enviable introduction into British cultural life!

The bodies of *Unteroffizier* Kurt Seydel and *Flieger* August Schleicher, one of whom was the crewman rescued with Helmut Pohle whom had died the next day from his injuries, and the other who had been brought out of the wreckage of Pohle's aircraft later, were buried on 20 October with full military honours in Portobello Cemetery. Their coffins, draped with the Swastika flag were kept overnight in St Philip's Church, before they were buried in a service attended by members of the auxiliary squadrons, and conducted by Squadron Leader the Reverend J. Rossie Brown, Edinburgh's padre to the RAF. Borne on trailers, the coffins were accompanied by sixty officers and men of the RAF. A firing party of ten sounded a volley over their graves while pipers from 603 Squadron's pipe band, played 'Over the Sea to Skye.' Air Vice-Marshal Richard Saul – the officer commanding No 13 Group Fighter Command – and Lord Provost Sir Henry Steele, joined the cortege as it passed along Brunstane Road and Milton Road, where thousands had gathered to pay their respects, or out of curiosity.

The Reverend J. Rossie Brown, who had been a tutor at St Andrew's University before the war, and who later accompanied the RAF to Canada, revealed a secret connected with the service he had held for the Forth Raiders, one Sunday after the war from his pulpit. He had written to the bereaved families via the International Red Cross, explaining that their sons had received a proper Christian burial, and that he regretted the loss of life so early in the hostilities. The secret was that he had never told anybody before that he had done this. On the 16th itself, the very same Reverend Rossie Brown had also manned one of the machine-gun posts at Turnhouse and had opened fire on one of the intruders that had flown close to the airfield. One of his uniformed parishoners noticed how short a burst he had sent towards the Hun. His reply was: 'Yes, it passed too quickly out of my diocese!'

Shortly after the raid the Reverend Rossie Brown visited Sigmund Storp and his two crew members in the military hospital at Edinburgh Castle. He found them to be 'very decent fellows', but was a trifle startled when on leaving, one of them gave him a Nazi salute.

There was something rather unwarlike about it all, as if the so-called 'Weekend Flyers' were still just sporting amateurs. But the squadrons soon got into their stride, guarding what the German crews came to call 'Suicide Corner'.

In February 1957, Hugh Dundas was attempting to track down the whereabouts of both Pohle and Storp. He already knew that Pohle had been promoted to Major in 1941 whilst in captivity and Storp to Captain in January 1940. As the men were at that time only 53 and 43 years of age, respectively, it seemed more than possible that they were still alive, either in Western Germany or Canada (if they stayed there after their release).

In due course Sigmund Storp, who had since become a Luftwaffe staff officer, Hanover district, was tracked down and interviewed.

Storp said it was of interest for him to cast his thoughts back seventeen years to the day when he became the first Luftwaffe man to be taken prisoner by the British. Storp had heard in hospital of the loss of a second machine – that of *Hauptmann* Pohle.

'That the Spitfires shot down only two machines was not the fault of the Spitfire pilots, but because of the late warning they received. Spitfire group pilots visited us the same day in hospital, bringing cigarettes and chocolate. We thought this very fair, and have not forgotten it to this day.' Being brought to London by train, Storp talked with an officer – and discovered it must have been the man who put Storp's motor out of action, thereby causing his crash. 'He told me his father had been shot down by Richthofen in the First World War. He invited me to have a drink in the dining-car.'

Storp did not know the man's name. In Canada Storp met Pohle, who was badly wounded in the head, but in 1957 he had no recent news of him. After treatment in Edinburgh, where Pohle's declined teeth had been straightened using a clamp, the German officer was taken to the Tower of London before being transferred to No 1 PoW camp at Grizedale Hall in Westmorland, and eventually to Canada. All of the Forth Raid prisoners had been kept in hospital for several weeks, not because their injuries were particularly bad, but because there was no place else to send them. Eventually they were issued with prisoner-of-war suits, which were in fact, civilian suits onto which brightly coloured patches had been sewn onto the back, elbows and thighs. These suits were supplied by the Co-op. The prisoners were amused by the fact that the size labels in their suits had a little border of very small swastikas. No doubt they looked upon this as a sign of good luck. The PoW camp, when they did eventually arrive, must have been a very lonely place to start with, but in the months that followed they soon began to fill with further unfortunates who came a cropper over Britain.

Later, Helmut Pohle did indeed return to Germany, and like his great adversary George Pinkerton, took to the farming life; the two men exchanged letters frequently. Pohle was due to come across to Scotland in 1989 as part of the centenary celebrations for the Forth Bridge. Unfortunately, however, shortly before this he broke his leg playing football with his grandchildren. Sadly, George Pinkerton and Pohle were due to meet for the first time since 1939 when George Pinkerton died in 1993.

Douglas Farquhar had an interesting letter that he showed Hugh Dundas which had come from Archie McKellar, dated 13 September 1940 and was in reply to one of his congratulating him after his famous destruction of three enemy aircraft with the same burst.

'Dear Douglas, Thanks very much for your letter; as I know you are interested and I hope that you do not think I'm shooting a line, herewith the reason. 605 were sent off to patrol May Island 20000. I was leading. Then we were vectored down to Newcastle and kept in the air and told to remain on patrol until running short of petrol. "A" flight lost us owing to the leader having engine trouble. I had just turned on to my reserve tank when lo and behold lots and lots of nasties. At last a chance to try our attacks, the rest you probably know, I got 3 destroyed and 1 possible (2 guns of De W) and the flight 8 destroyed and 3 probable. I can assure you however when I had a phone message from AOC I was shaken to the core. You will notice my new address (Croydon) and I would be delighted if you can come over and see us soon, it is out of the question for me just now as I have to lead the squadron.

'Walter Churchill was slightly wounded on Wednesday. We arrived here on Saturday, went in to our fight on Sunday but played for caution. We attacked the bombers and managed to turn them but did not repeat our attack owing to very heavy fighter escort. One of our pilots down in flames but safe. On Monday another big show; on this occasion I had the most astonishing luck, one 109 yellow-nosed little bugger, and then I took the section head-on into the leader of the bomber formation. Some 110s jumped us and got my No 3, missing. No 2, a Polish boy turned on them. I fired at the leader of the formation, saw smoke and flame from each wing, fired at his left-hand machine and shot his wing off, at the same time No 1 exploded and took his No 2 with him in flames. Believe it or not, all confirmed 1,200 rounds fired. We had another show on Wednesday and I had a fair amount of luck once more; however no more line-shooting. Did you hear that Sandy (Johnstone then CO 602) got the DFC and that Roger Coverley and Harry Moody are both missing and Paul (Webb) and Glynn (Ritchie) are both in hospital with slight wounds. 602 have certainly given a big shock to the Teutons. Yours aye Archie.'

Just a few weeks after writing this letter, Archie McKellar who had played such an important part in bringing down Helmut Pohle's Ju 88 on 16 October 1939, and who was largely responsible for the first aircraft to be brought down on mainland Britain, was killed. John Young, Battle of Britain Fighter Association historian told me: 'I met Archie McKellar in East Lothian I remember clearly him saying to me "John, How's the love around here" I was unable to answer – we had been very busy!'

CHAPTER ELEVEN

INADEQUACIES AND ACCOLADE

The joint communique issued by the Admiralty, Air Ministry and Ministry for Home Security read:

'This afternoon about 2.30 a series of bombing raids began. These were directed at the ships lying in the Forth and were conducted by about a dozen machines. No serious damage was done to any of His Majesty's ships.

'One bomb glanced off the cruiser *Southampton*, causing slight damage near her bow, and sank the Admiral's barge and pinnace which were moored empty alongside.

'There were three casualties on board the *Southampton* and seven aboard the cruiser *Edinburgh*. Another bomb fell near the destroyer *Mohawk*. This bomb burst on the water and the splinters caused 25 casualties to the men on the deck of the destroyer. Only superficial damage was caused to the vessel, which, like the others is ready for sea.'

An official account was consequently issued to the press for publication, on Tuesday, 17 October, stating:

'Victory over the first German bombers to raid Great Britain since the war began has been largely shared in by men who, a few weeks ago, were Scottish stockbrokers, lawyers, and sheep farmers. At least two of the four enemy raiders accounted for during Monday's raid on the Forth were shot down by British fighter aircraft. They beat off the raiders in such a way that not more than half the German aircraft are believed to have returned home. About twelve or fourteen bombers took part in the raid. Apart from four which were brought down by British fighters, and anti-aircraft, and naval gunfire, several are thought to have been too crippled to complete the passage of the North Sea. No pilot claims to have brought down one of

129

Monday's raiders single-handed. Their defeat was a team job. One running fight began over the Pentland Hills. British fighters chased a German bomber away from the Pentlands, and it crashed into the sea off Port Seton. Shots from several aircraft helped to cripple it, but the "coup de grâce" was delivered by an auxiliary pilot who, before the war practised as a lawyer. He had taken a bet that he would be the first member of his squadron to bring down a German plane. Swooping low over Edinburgh, a Squadron Leader, who was a stock-broker in civil life, chased another enemy raider out to sea. Two other members of his squadron, a sheep farmer and the manager of a firm of plasterers, shot down a bomber off Crail.'

Bear in mind that this report was issued to the press long before any of the real facts had been released, and it becomes quite comical in its inaccuracies. Unfortunately, statements like this do an awful lot of harm when we try to research history. If an official account states that four aircraft were brought down, then all the newspapers in Scotland, Great Britain, indeed the world, will report that four aircraft were brought down. And unfortunately, even though in the days which followed, the truth slowly emerged, that only two aircraft had been shot down, people have a tendency to remember the first story they hear. As for the professions with which the pilots were accredited: Gifford was a solicitor, so yes, I suppose 'lawyer' would be acceptable: true, Archie McKellar was an apprentice plasterer in his father's business, but to call him the manager might have annoyed the old man a trot: as for Pinkerton, not doubt he was a trifle miffed to be termed a 'sheep farmer', although no doubt 'Sheep' Gilroy saw the funny side of it.

The Scottish Auxiliaries received accolades from near and far, when their success was made public. There was score upon score of congratulatory messages. Senior officers of the RAF, the Royal Navy, and the Army sent their tributes. There were messages from ships at sea, and from many other squadrons of both the Auxiliary and Royal Air Forces. One unit telegraphed to 603 Squadron: 'Nice work, boys. Turrnhoose uber Alles.' Another squadron addressed its message to the 'Hun Crashers, Edinburgh.'

For some of those involved, 16 October 1939 was a howling success; for others it presented a 'fog'. The term 'fog' basically means the softening of bad news, or covering over a blunder. Often it was extended to a total blackout of news on a major disaster like the sinking of a warship with heavy losses – after all, public morale had to be protected.

German radio issued the following account: 'On Monday between 2.30 and 3.15p.m., German bombers made a successful attack on British warships in the Firth of Forth.'

'Two British cruisers were hit, in spite of tremendous efforts on the part of the British Air Force to repulse the attackers.'

'Two British chaser planes were shot down and two German planes are missing.' Their claim to have shot down two Spitfires was of course a complete fabrication. In fact, truth be known, some of the Auxiliaries suffered more through running into flocks of peewits over the shoreline, than through enemy action.

Quite possibly the disaster elements outweigh the jubilation of 602 and 603 Squadrons, who emerged as the only real victors that day; and of course the Auxiliary Air Force itself.

To some extent we have already discussed the inadequacies of the German plan. Not just the highly questionable sources of their intelligence; which would appear to have been little or no intelligence at all in certain circumstances. Also the inadequacies in the aircraft they continued to send on missions over Scotland and the north-east corner of England. Basically, when facing the possibility of being intercepted by Spitfires or Hurricanes, flying a Heinkel He 111, Dornier Do 17Z, or Junkers Ju 87B, was tantamount to aerial suicide. In some ways the Luftwaffe had little or no alternative, especially when trying to adhere to the unrealistic demands of Hitler and Göring. When allowed to attack practically unmolested by the enemy – as the Luftwaffe had been able to do in their previous campaigns such as in Poland – the Junkers was absolutely superb for use in locations like the Firth of Forth or Scapa Flow. Their limitation however was in their fighter capability, and they were no match for the British machines. It was nearly impossible for Messerschmitts of any description to accompany these northern missions because of their limitations on fuel. When it came to the crunch, the bomber pilots were on their own and that's why this part of Britain soon earned the nickname 'Suicide Corner'. The type of aircraft that the Luftwaffe used on that first raid against the Firth of Forth, the Junkers Ju 88, tended to fair slightly better than all the other bombers over Britain. Its high-speed diving capability and considerable manoeuvrability meant, that while it could not stand up to the British fighters in combat, it could certainly evade them. This probably helps to account for the fact that only two planes were shot down that day. It was also a sturdy aircraft that could withstand considerable battle damage. However, when not afforded the protection of a fighter escort, it was only marginally more successful and was still easy prey for the RAF and AAF.

The other disastrous thing about the raid as far as the Germans were concerned, was the loss of two of their top pilots and many senior aircrew. Although they had managed to score a surprise attack they

131

seem to have wasted the opportunity. Below them lay the British fleet; veritable sitting ducks. Not one single bomb scored a decisive hit and the damage they caused was negligible. Their only real success would have been in the deaths of Captain Jolly and his crew aboard the *Mohawk*, and on reflection this would only have been a success over British morale and resolve.

At the end of the day, no matter how much we may harp on about the inadequacies of the Germans, we would do well to remember the inadequacies of our own defence mechanism as well. How, in 1939, with the entire country covered by a spider's web of Observer Corps posts which had spotted and tracked the intruders, much of the east coast surveyed by a radar screen, and two fighter squadrons at readiness literally a few miles and minutes away, were German bombers allowed – in broad daylight and on a relatively sunny afternoon – to cross the coast, cover some sixty or so miles of Scottish countryside, and bomb the Royal Navy, before somebody eventually twigged that those Blenheims were in actual fact Nazi bombers on a deadly mission. Quite frankly, it does not bear thinking about. Among other things it later emerged that our own fighters had on various occasions, been sent directly away from the locations that they should have been investigating because of plotting errors. Six training aircraft from RNAS Donibristle had been identified as the enemy by a searchlight detachment at Dunbar and an AA battery, which accounted for another waste of vital resources.

Another incredible fact is that 603 Squadron alone, exhausted 16,000 rounds of ammunition that day – 602 presumably a similar amount – all for the destruction of only two enemy aircraft.

John Kerr who was a gunner on HMS *Mohawk* and who was wounded by the explosion that killed Captain Jolly and several of his mates, feels bitter towards the Royal Air Force.

'Had we just got a bit of warning we could have got to our action stations and had the RAF got into the air in time we might have saved a lot of lives.

'Instead, we were all caught unawares. We certainly did not get the cover we should have had. We read reports about how the RAF chased the raiders and that everyone was on the ball – it is absolute rubbish. It's time to put the record straight. Edinburgh's 603 Squadron who downed the first enemy aircraft of the war over Britain – one of the Forth raiders – said that some radar detection installations were not very efficient and there might have been a bit of complacency on the part of the Observer Corps. It was a terrible mistake to make so early in the war. I think there will always be a different story to tell about this bloomer. I can assure you there was no action before they tried to bomb us, and the RAF was not to be seen anywhere, or I would not have been going for a shower ready for shore leave. We would have been closed-up at action stations. I still feel bitter about it and the RAF took all the praise. I know 603 made a name for themselves later in the war, as we did. But we lost a lot of boys that day, needlessly. I went frequently to visit their graves, where I could still see my old mates. I would break down and cry; I am 75 years old next birthday.'

Although we can sympathise with John Kerr, and feel a sadness for those who lost their lives, there in no question that 602 or 603 Squadrons weren't on the ball. Every available aircraft that afternoon was in the air searching relentlessly for a sign of the raiders. The pilots were themselves, victims of circumstances beyond their control. Like any soldiers, sailors or airmen, they obeyed orders. If pilots were ordered to investigate 'Bogeys' at Point A, while the real 'Bandits' were actually at Point B, I do not think they can be held responsible for the fact that they were in the wrong place.

Many people I have spoken with, and many recorded accounts of the day, seem to accuse the Observer Corps of being negligent in the accuracy and speed of their information. In truth, this again was far from being the case. I have heard many people talk about an Observer Corps post on the Isle of May and the resident Observer's complacency. Royal Observer Corps records indicate quite clearly that there was no Observer Corps post on the island at that time. The transport problem of ferrying volunteer Observers back and forth every twelve hours would have been a logistical nightmare.

On the question of the warning given, the raiders were initially located by radar which then went off air, due to reasons that we have already established. However, although Drone Hill was down, the raiders were still continually tracked by other radar stations along the east coast. The aircraft were then located by the Observer Corps, correctly recognised and tracked by the posts of 31 Group, Galashiels and 36 Group, Dunfermline. There is absolutely no question at all, that the Observer Corps were lacking in any way. The problem was that Fighter Command received observations and intelligence from a number of other sources, such as search-light crews and anti-aircraft batteries. History has been inclined to group all of these observers under the Observer Corps' umbrella, when they were anything but. The mistakes made by these other sources have therefore traditionally been blamed on the Observer Corps. When an observer from a search-light crew sent the fighters the wrong way, the word that sticks in people's memories is 'observer' not 'search-light'; and to

133

everybody concerned that meant the Observer Corps.

Sir Hugh Dowding was so pleased with the Corps' performance on that day that he sent the following message to the Corps: 'I am very pleased with the way in which the Observer Corps acquitted themselves in this, the first action of the war in which they are able to take part. The visibility conditions were difficult and the bomber formation split up into individual aircraft. In the circumstances I consider that the Observer Corps operated with great efficiency and I should like all concerned to be informed accordingly.'

An accolade of this nature would never have been issued if the Observer Corps had failed in its duty. So the fact remains that the enemy aircraft had been seen, identified and tracked. And yet, no alarm was raised in Edinburgh. The first sirens to sound at the airfields, as the fighter pilots themselves who took part are witness, such as Sandy Johnstone, did not sound until the raid was in progress. The error seems to have happened somewhere between the two. But none of this helps to explain why no sirens were sounded in the city itself, even while German aircraft were hopping over the roof-tops of Portobello.

16 October 1939 was a very important day in the history of the Second World War, a great deal hinged on its success for both camps. However, its relevance has always been played down, and I can only imagine that this was due to the embarrassment caused to the government and the powers that be within the Air Defence of our country at the time. Happily, the mistakes which occurred that day, were corrected, and by the time of the Battle of Britain, the following summer, Air Chief Marshal Dowding, the Commander-in-Chief of Fighter Command, was able to field one of the most comprehensive early warning systems the world has ever known. Every part of that mechanism played a valuable part in our eventual victory over the Luftwaffe. On 16 October 1939, mistakes were made. Perhaps ultimately those mistakes were beneficial. When it came down to the very survival of our nation, perhaps even the survival of civilisation itself, mistakes were few and far between.

The day after the raid, 1 KG 30 was in action again, this time led by a new commander, *Hauptmann* Dench. Dench, who took over from the imprisoned Helmut Pohle, led four Ju 88s against Scapa Flow.

After this raid and further attempts by the Germans to sink the British ships at Rosyth and Scapa Flow, the Royal Navy decided that the situation on the east coast was getting a little too hot to handle. Instead, many of the ships were relocated to bases in the west. This remained the situation until the RAF and the RNAS were able to provide a suitable fighter blanket over the whole area.

Also on the day after the raid, 602 Squadron was sent a request for one of the pilots who took part in the fighting to travel south to RAF Northolt and join a tactical course at the Fighter Development School, presumably to relate his experiences.

Douglas Farquhar decided to send Sandy Johnstone, who always considered himself undeserving of the task, as he felt that out of all the pilots who had taken part, his had been the least significant contribution to the outcome. As it turned out, it didn't really matter anyway, as nobody on the course seemed particularly interested in Johnstone or what had happened at the Forth. Perhaps the 'fog' had got there before him. Or perhaps, because he was an Auxiliary, he was jealously 'pooh-poohed'!

One positive thing to come out of the Forth raid, was improvements to the Balloon Barrage around the coast of Great Britain. In all the accounts I have read and heard about the Forth raid, I do not think I have ever heard the word 'balloon' mentioned once. Balloons were important to the protection of both military and civilian targets. They were particularly useful against dive-bombers, such as the Ju 88. This type of aircraft dived from a great height, releasing its bombs low over the target, at a crucial moment, just before beginning to pull out of the dive. The altitude at which the bombs were ejected, roughly corresponded to the height of the balloon barrage, or even lower still. This meant that as the dive-bomber pulled up, it would inevitably crash into the lethal cables which held the balloon aloft. On 16 October there would appear to have been a criminal lack of such defences over the Forth.

Major A. P. Le M. Skinkinson OBE MA, wrote at the time: 'The speed with which the location of balloons can be changed was well demonstrated when German aircraft attempted a bombing raid over the Forth Bridge in October 1939. As there were no balloons defending this vital transport link at the time, a complete barrage was hauled down in Glasgow and with the aid of special trains and the splendid co-operation of the crews, it was flying again within 24 hours over the Firth of Forth.' Very commendable indeed! But why the hell weren't there any balloons protecting the area in the first place, when it must have been pretty obvious, especially after the sinking of the *Royal Oak* at Scapa Flow, that Rosyth and the Forth Rail Bridge were potential targets for the Luftwaffe?

In 1940 the GPO Film Unit made a film which showed men of the Auxiliary Air Force Balloon Squadrons, training and working. The film, entitled 'Squadron 992', directed by Alberto Cavalcanti and starring officers and men of the Royal Air Force, included an excellent reconstruction of the air raid on 16 October 1939. The film captures the atmosphere perfectly and shows a misty morning around the Forth Bridge, where people carry on their everyday activities. A group of soldiers play football; fishermen put out to sea; and two poachers meander into the quiet Lothian countryside with their dog. The following sequence has some remarkable footage of the Forth Bridge itself, taken from the air, as though through the eyes of the Nazi pilots as they home-in on the Royal Navy ships. Sailors rush to their action stations, anti-aircraft guns open up, and bullets dance along the street, where the soldiers who had been playing football, dive for cover.

Perhaps the most poignant moment of the film is when the two poachers are seen in a field as their dog courses a hare. Suddenly they become aware of the German aircraft overhead, being chased by a Spitfire. As the aeroplanes twist and turn, the action flashes between the combat in the sky and the desperate last few moments of the hare's futile bid to escape. As the hare is finally brutally caught and killed, we next see the image of the three German airmen drifting in the North Sea, clinging helplessly to an air float. The fishermen pull them on to their vessel. After this vivid and extremely factual reconstruction the commentary explains: 'The raiders had failed, but the enemy had shown his hand. The coast, the harbours, the estuaries, were to be his target. Right away it was decided to extend our great balloon barrage by hundreds of miles to lay traps all around our sea coast. Within an hour orders had come through for a new barrage to guard the Forth. Every balloon squadron is completely mobile and self-contained. Three hours later Squadron 992 and a great convoy of fifty lorries, winches, hydrogen trailers, maintenance vans and store trucks, pulled out and headed north. Their training finished, they were on a real job at last.'

John Dickson the skipper of the yawl *Dayspring,* which rescued Sigmund Storp and his crew, took part in the filming of *Squadron 992,* which was shot on a Saturday afternoon east of Inchkeith as the water off Port Seton was too rough. One Jack Nicholson of Port Seton, a medical student, featured in the film as a German – as he had blond hair!

Quite possibly the hardest thing of all about writing this book, was trying to decide in my own mind, exactly what happened, what was the truth and what was heresay and resultant myth. There were so many contradictions to cope with. Even the actual date of the raid caused a deal of confusion when I started out. A number of people in the Edinburgh area insisted that the raid took place on the 17th not the 16th. I was confident that I had the right date but as more and more people told me I was wrong, I sincerely began to doubt my sources. I decided to look in the first history book I could lay my hands on to make sure they were wrong. Confusion added to confusion, when the first book I picked up, also reported the raid to have taken place on the 17th. This happened to be a coincidence. All other material I have since read, confirmed the date as being the 16th. And of course, the final proof is from the diaries of the fighter pilots like Sandy Johnstone and Jim Morton, who were actually there; as well as the reports from the Observer Corps, police, and squadron records etc.

One confusion resolved, there was also the point as to whether the aircraft were Heinkels, Ju 88s, or a combination of the two. Sigmund Storp, Helmut Pohle and Horst von Riesen, who carried out the raid, were all Ju 88 men. However, dozens of people who sent letters to me, or whom I spoke with, had seen Heinkels. In fact, no eye witness has ever told me he saw a Junkers. Few people in Britain had even heard of a Ju 88, so it is unlikely they would have been identified as such. When you consider that many of these eye-witnesses were only children at the time and these were the very first German aircraft that they had ever seen, I very much doubt that they would have known what they were. Remember that even some of the professionals confused them as being our own Blenheims, until it was too late. If a few days after the raid, or even weeks after the raid, those eye-witnesses had heard somebody say to them that the aircraft were Heinkels, then from that day forth, and fifty years later, they would be adamant that that was exactly what they had seen.

What I am sure of is that a lot of people when asked about the first air raid on mainland Britain and the day the first enemy aircraft was shot down, actually confuse this event with another day. The two days in question are so closely connected that this confusion is quite understandable, and has contributed to the difficulties encountered while researching this book. A number of people told me, 'Yes, I remember 16 October 1939 very well'. They go on to describe the raid in some detail; tell stories of how the aircraft had flown low over Edinburgh; tell of how 603 and 602 Squadrons had chased them; even explain how Archie McKellar and Patsy Gifford had brought down the enemy. However, when it comes to the point when the aircraft should cross the coast and drop into the Forth, the story suddenly changes. The aircraft they had seen turns inland and comes down in the Lammermuir Hills near Haddington in East Lothian. This incident actually happened on 28 October 1939, twelve days after the first mainland raid. However, it is important because the aircraft in question was the first German aircraft actually shot down on mainland Britain. This then is where the confusion lies. When you ask someone if they remember 16 October, the day the first enemy aircraft was shot down over Britain, they immediately remember the second incident and relate it with the date of the first. Patsy Gifford and Archie McKellar got so much praise in those few weeks, that their names have become inseparable from both incidents. In fact during the twelve days that elapsed between the shooting down of Pohle and Storp and the subsequent shooting down of the Heinkel near Haddington; the Germans sent other raids against the Forth which were seen off by the combined efforts of 602 and 603 Squadrons.

The following account of what happened on 22 October 1939 comes from the diary of Jim Morton:

'22 October 1939. Fine. Cloud 8/10. 3,000 feet. Hazy. Light westerly wind.

'1600: Red Section to patrol five miles north of St Abb's Head.

'Failed to start engine immediately and lost Patsy Gifford and Robertson in the haze. After tally-ho from Robertson, saw enemy pursued by two Spitfires flying north about three miles away and climbing to a bank of cloud. Followed them, and kept below base of cloud turning east as being probable course of enemy. At the end of the bank of cloud, enemy emerged about half a mile from me with two Spitfires above and to port of him. One peeled off and attacked in gaps of cloud without breaking away between bursts. When he finished, I went in as the other Spitfire had disappeared. Came in from astern and fired burst of 8–10 seconds from No 1 position. Enemy was now in clear sky above wispy cloud. After my attack, he swung round to port and started to lose height. Attacked again, and as return fire had ceased, went in to close range and fired the rest of my ammunition. After my first attack, Patsy exhorted me to – "For God's sake be careful with your pellets, I have none left". After the second attack, the enemy came down quite quickly in a glide back towards the coast. He made a nice landing in the sea and three of them clambered out into a rubber boat. I thought he put down his wheels on the glide, but have been pooh-poohed. They were up when he landed. We flew round a convoy to try and get an escort to go to the dinghy and then came home at full speed. "I have shot down one Dornier," periodically on the RT from Patsy. Enemy was actually an He 111. On landing, found I had a bullet in the sump and less than half a gallon of oil left out of 5½ gallons. Workshops say two minutes more would have seen the engine solid. It was very fortunate I did not know about it at the time and I shall be very careful not to play about 10 to 15 miles out to sea after the next one. This affair of my engine just shows how impossible it is to try and say who is responsible for the death of the bomber unless it comes down like a high pheasant. Everyone is very disappointed at the effect of our fire. The general idea seems to be that the gun pattern is far too open, and Patsy has got us on to drawing lots of circles to see how the harmonisation can be improved.'

Regarding this particular incident, the 603 Squadron Benevolent Fund booklet said: 'Less than a week after the Forth raid an Edinburgh section had shot down a Heinkel 111 into the sea seven miles off land. Three of the crew of four were seen to take to their collapsible dinghy. They paddled hard and waved frantically. After refuelling, the Spitfires returned to the scene and directed the rescue of the derelicts by HMS *Gurkha*. One Spitfire had received a bullet in the oil sump, of which the pilot was blissfully unaware. When he landed at base, he had exactly half a gallon of oil remaining.'

On 28 October, Flying Officer Archie McKellar had the distinction of being the first pilot to bring down a German aircraft on mainland Britain during the Second World War. The Heinkel He 111 made impact close to the Longyester-Humbie road near Kidlaw Farm, Gifford, East Lothian. The pilot was wounded and his Observer, although unhurt was in a state of shock; the other two crew members were killed.

A large crowd of people saw the final moments of the chase and the consequent crash, and naturally, many were also to visit the crash site to view the wreckage. So as you can see, the striking similarities which connect all of these early successes have added to the misrepresentation of facts and common confusion over dates which have persisted down through the years.

George Mullay, who still lives in Edinburgh recalled:

'I was nine years old and was playing with some pals in a big concrete playpark near Pilrig when a Heinkel 111 bomber flew low over us. Before we knew where we were, the Heinkel gunners began firing at us! As the bullets spat all around, we took to our heels hardly believing what was happening. We were probably the first British civilians to be shot at by the enemy.

'The raider was shot down to the east of Edinburgh, and I remember watching the funeral procession of the crew who had shot at me. They were buried in Portobello Cemetery. I was later given the collar rank-badges from the Germans' uniforms and the identification plate from the shot down Heinkel. I still have them.'

These unusual mementoes were given to George Mullay by his father who had been a mechanic at Turnhouse at the time of the raid.

An eye-witness to the crash, Mr John Irvine, who lived on a nearby farm, was interviewed by the BBC shortly afterwards, and said:

'I am the grieve at Longnewton Farm, close behind the Lammermoor Hill. I was filling up sacks of barley about a quarter past ten when I heard a noise like the hurling of a barrow. That's what I thought it was at first, but it went on and came nearer, and then I knew it was the noise of guns. Then we saw a big black machine with two engines coming over the trees from the north-west. There were four British machines with it. They were circling all round and rattling bullets into the German as hard as they could do it.

'I thought we ought to take cover – there were women workers there. But curiosity brought us out again – while we were running in and out – so that we saw the German go over the houses, so low that it almost touched the chimneys. Then they all went out of sight up over the hill, and a few minutes later I saw our fighters going back – all four of them. They seemed to be finished with their job. So we ran up the hill to see what had happened.

'Two of the crew were dead. I expect they would be the gunners, and they must have been shot before they came my length because I never saw them firing at our planes. The machine had scraped its tail over a dyke and come down on the moor on an even keel. One of the crew wasn't hurt at all. He was pulling out his mate. By the time we got up he had him drawn out and lying on the ground.

'We tried to talk to the unwounded man, but he didn't know what we were saying. But he spoke a little English. The wounded man wanted a drink, but the doctor said he ought not to have one. He had two bullet-wounds in the back.

'The police took the unwounded man away. Before he went he shook hands with his mate. We got a gate off one of the fences and carried the wounded man down to the road, and waited there till the ambulance came for him.'

A 603 Squadron source stated that the Heinkel was probably the most 'ventilated' target ever attacked by Spitfire fighters. There was scarcely a part of its wings, fuselage, and tail unit that did not bear evidence of Browning bullets.

One amazing fact is that although Edinburgh seemed to attract so much of the Luftwaffe's attention in those early days, casualties from the city during the war were extremely light. Only 20 people were killed, and 218 injured, during air attacks on the city. There were small towns in the south of England that lost more. Glasgow however, suffered 1,927 deaths. There is a story, the entire truth of which I am not in a position to confirm, that on the whole of Clydebank, only twelve houses survived the war without some damage caused by air attack. I wouldn't be at all surprised though, if the story isn't very near to the truth. The worst damage caused to Edinburgh through an air attack, surprisingly came from a single bomb, dropped from a lone raider on a bonded store in Duff Street. The burning spirit caused an immense inferno that could be seen from all over the city.

You may recall that very early in the book Marcus Robinson of 602 Squadron insisted that there was no rivalry between the Scottish Auxiliaries. After the Forth Raid there was almost certainly an element of rivalry. In this book the whole raid has been mapped out as it happened, and we know where and when the first two aircraft were shot down. When Patsy Gifford and George Pinkerton returned to their respective bases that afternoon, both pilots would almost certainly have thought they were the first. The question was not decided in a hurry, and it was not until 24 January 1942 that an official answer to the question was provided from Headquarters, Fighter Command, which read: 'Claims of 602 and 603 Squadrons ref destruction of first enemy aircraft. (1) With reference to the above subject, it has now been established that the first enemy aircraft to be destroyed by Fighter Command was shot down by 603 Squadron at 14.45 hours on 16th October 1939. 602 Squadron destroyed an enemy aircraft at 15.00 hours on the same day. (2) 603 Squadron therefore has the honour of destroying the first enemy aircraft during the war.'

It seems that even after this official report was produced, the controversy continued. On 5 March 1943 a letter was sent from Headquarters No 11 Group, at Uxbridge to Mr J. Nerney, who was at that time the librarian at the Air Ministry. The letter stated that the City of Edinburgh was producing a booklet about No 603 Squadron, in connection with 'Wings for Victory Week'. The Lord Provost, who was Honorary Air Commodore of the Squadron, was anxious to obtain an official statement to the effect that 603 Squadron had the honour of destroying the first enemy aircraft to attack this country. Enclosed with the letter were copies of the first three combat reports of the Forth Raid, from which could be seen that 603 Squadron got their Hun fifteen minutes before 602. Ten days later on 15 March 1943, came the reply:

'Two contestants for the honour of having shot down the first enemy aircraft over Great Britain arises in the persons of (1) Flight Lieutenant G.C. Pinkerton of 602 Squadron, and (2) Flight Lieutenant P. Gifford of 603 Squadron. The operation is the same in both cases, namely a raid by enemy aircraft on the Firth of Forth on October 16th, 1939.

'With regard to the first claimant, Flight Lieutenant Pinkerton, the

Operations Record Book of 602 Squadron shows on Form 540 that the section to which he belonged, took off at 14.23 hours and landed again at 15.15 hours. Form 541 of the same record gives his time of taking off as 14.25 hours and his landing at 15.00 hours. In his Combat report Flight Lieutenant Pinkerton gives the time of his attack on the enemy aircraft as "about 15.00 hours".

'In the case of the second claimant, the Operation Record Book for 603 Squadron, Form 541, gives the time of Flight Lieutenant Gifford's taking off as 14.30 hours and his landing as 14.55 hours. Form 540 does not record individual times. In his Combat Report Gifford gives his time of attack as 14.45 hours.

'On the evidence which the records give, the claim of 603 Squadron in the person of Flight Lieutenant Gifford should be upheld because of the definiteness of the time given.

'Flight Lieutenant Pinkerton's claim, on the other hand, suffers on account of discrepancies in times given on Form 540 and 541 and on account of his loose statement in his Combat Report. "About 15.00 hours". It is hardly to be expected that in this short action Pinkerton would have misjudged to the extent of 15 minutes, which is the difference in time in dispute.'

So in 1943, that was the Air Ministry's official line. However, the most concrete evidence comes from the Observer Corps Post at Crail, where an eye-witness account stated: 'Plane shot down in sea three miles off Crail at 14.55. Plane was going east, chased by two fighters.' This report reduces the Air Ministry's fifteen minute differential, to only ten minutes, and I think beyond a shadow of a doubt establishes Patsy Gifford as the first pilot to shoot down an enemy aircraft over Britain during the Second World War.

603 Squadron's Operations Record Book for the 16 October quite clearly logs Spitfire L.1070 (XT-A), flown by Flight Lieutenant P. Gifford, back into Turnhouse at 14.55. This was actually five minutes before Colin Robertson and Ken MacDonald, the rest of Red Section. So, if the Observer Corps at Crail saw Helmut Pohle's Ju 88 crash into the sea at 14.55, and Patsy Gifford was already back on the ground at that time, I think that proves conclusively that (solicitor) Gifford wins the day. Case closed!

CHAPTER TWELVE

IN THE LIGHT OF
EXPERIENCE GAINED

Nearly every account of the Forth Raid I have read makes at least one basic error, the common one being an exaggeration of the number of aircraft actually brought down, or their type. Even Winston Churchill in *The Gathering Storm* published in 1948, says of the attack: 'Twelve or more machines in flights of two or three at a time bombed our cruisers lying in the Firth. Twenty-five officers and sailors were killed or wounded; but four enemy bombers were brought down, three by our fighter squadrons and one by anti-aircraft.'

An article in *The Scotsman* on Tuesday 17 October 1939 said: 'Three of the raiders were destroyed by the RAF. One was brought down in the sea near Port Seton, another crashed in the sea off Crail, and a third was destroyed in the Pentland Hills. The fourth plane was brought down by anti-aircraft fire, crashing in flames behind a wood at North Queensferry.'

A number of more realistic accounts put the bag down to three; the two we already know about and a third one that went down 'somewhere off the Northumberland coast'. There is an element of truth to this particular story, but the aircraft in question was a Heinkel He 111, which was sent over the following day to undertake a photo reconnaissance of the results of the Forth Raid. After ditching, the Heinkel transmitted an S.O.S. to Westerland, in the hope of assistance. The distress signal was duly answered by a Nazi flying boat. Its approach was observed from the shore, and a little later Spitfires were overhead and had forced it down. The crews of both aircraft were taken prisoner. There was slight confusion due to the fact that the Heinkel pilot insisted he had been shot down by Spitfires. It transpired in fact that he had actually been shot down by Gladiators, and was too ashamed to admit that he had been shot down by biplanes.

The question of why the air raid sirens did not sound in Edinburgh was tackled by the Prime Minister in the House of Commons the day after the raid:

'As the attack was local and appeared to be developing only on a small scale, and as our defences were fully ready, it was not considered appropriate in this particular instance to issue an air raid warning, which would have caused dislocation and inconvenience over a wide area. The responsibility for issuing air raid warnings must be left to the competent authorities, but the circumstances in which warnings had been issued would be carefully reviewed in the light of the experience gained.'

Mr Mathers the Labour MP for Linlithgow then asked:

'Can the Prime Minister say anything about the fact that a train was allowed on the Forth Bridge, which was obviously an object of attack, during the time these air raids were in progress, and whether anything is to be done to prevent that sort of thing happening in future, and also whether consideration is being given to the facts arising out of this air raid and to the representation that has been made for some time by South Queensferry Town Council, to have that burgh looked upon as an area which should be evacuated? Will consideration now be given more seriously to that question than has been the case up to the present?'

The Prime Minister replied:

'I do not think we know all the circumstances in which trains were permitted across the bridge, but that, of course, will be taken into consideration too. With regard to the other question, I should like notice.'

The newspapers of the day were less than happy with the Prime Minister's explanation of the absence of air raid warnings, deeming them 'unsatisfactory' and 'incomprehensible'. Regarding the Premier's undertaking that 'the circumstances in which warnings are to be issued, will be carefully reviewed in the light of experience gained', the *Daily Record* said: 'It is surely a reasonable assumption that, in effecting the necessary reform of existing arrangements, those people on the spot should be armed with the responsibility and power to decide on air raid warnings in their own area, rather than be dependent for sanction or instructions on some competent authority at a distance.'

On the same subject *The Scotsman* wrote: 'The truth is that the competent authority was extraordinarily fortunate over Monday's experience, and only the lucky fact that there was no loss of civilian life –

as there might have been – and no serious damage to property – as there might have been – have saved it. What would have been done to the competent authority if, for example, a bomb had been dropped on a train passing over the Forth Bridge, as might have happened? If it is wise, the competent authority will not cease to bless its good fortune, and take the escape to heart.'

Lord Provost Sir Henry Steele, who had a personal score to settle, was not satisfied with the Prime Minister's explanations either. Afterwards he said:

'The question of responsibility for no warnings being given was discussed at a meeting of the Edinburgh ARP Committee yesterday. The meeting was held, as usual, in private, and it was considered inadvisable at that stage for the Committee to issue a statement on the matter. No official view was obtainable regarding Mr Chamberlain's explanation in the House of Commons, and the Committee felt that as the matter was now the subject of Home Office investigation it was not competent for them to make any statement. It was apparently the feeling of the Committee, however, that the matter could safely be left where the responsibility lay – namely, the Air Ministry and the Edinburgh Fighter Command.

'It is understood the question was also raised as to whether or not the Edinburgh authorities should have acted on their own initiative. The discussion indicated that it was the general feeling of the Committee that, as the country was at war, the authorities in Edinburgh must loyally play their part as members of the Home Defence organisation, and abide by the orders which had been laid down by higher authorities. The general public, it was considered, would readily appreciate the confusion which was almost certain to arise should there by any departure from a unified command.

'Reports continue to be received of civilians in Edinburgh having narrow escapes from being struck by shell splinters or machine-gun bullets during the raid. One of these reports comes from Portobello where three bullets have been found in a house. One of the bullets hit a chair in which an elderly man, who had been an invalid for years, usually sat. The man was in bed at the time, as he had not been feeling well that morning. Another bullet smashed a chandelier.'

It is amazing that he did not actually mention his own display cabinet which is presumably what he had on his mind, in a round-about fashion.

On the subject of sirens *The Scotsman* noted: 'An amazing feature of the attack was that many places, including Edinburgh, sounded no air raid sirens, and people stood in the streets gazing up at aerial dogfights, unaware that it was the real thing. Even officers of the defence forces were for a time under the impression that all the planes were British. One explanation of the absence of warning was that earlier there had been British bombing practice on the Forth.'

Another point of view was that the decision not to sound the sirens until it became quite clear that the civilian population would be endangered had been taken because the Germans had been sending solitary reconnaissance planes flying along the east coast. When the sirens went the factories had to close down until the 'all-clear' was sounded, which was disrupting productivity.

The various police authorities in the area, who were responsible for sounding local alarms made their own reports. Inspector Maclean's report from South Queensferry Police Station, to the Chief Constable stated:

> 'No Air Raid Messages were received and the first intimation of the air raid was machine-gun fire from an aeroplane followed by the explosion of a bomb being dropped in the vicinity of the Forth Bridge. The siren at Port Edgar then sounded, followed by the local signal on the Distillery siren, and bomb explosions and the noise of anti-aircraft gun fire from the local units. What is believed to be the "tail" of an enemy plane fell east of the Forth Bridge into the water, and floated north-westwards.'

This was probably the canopy of either Helmut Pohle's Ju 88, which had been ripped off during his dive-attack, or the canopy from one of the other aircraft. This apparently was a common fault with the Ju 88 at that time, which was remedied soon afterwards.

> 'The actual raid in the first place would last about 50 or 60 minutes, and about 3.50p.m. the "Raiders Passed" signal was sounded at Port Edgar, followed by the same signal on the local siren. About 4p.m., however, the signals sounded the Air Raid Warnings and a plane was sighted over Port Edgar but was driven off by Anti-Aircraft Gun Fire from the surrounding batteries and the two warships.
>
> 'It has now been ascertained that a 2 lb anti-aircraft cartridge was picked up, unexploded, in the drive about 400 yards east of Leuchold House, Dalmeny, and two anti-aircraft shells were found, also unexploded, at Kirkliston, one on Almondhill Road and the other on the street at the Cross Roads in the village. These shells have been attended to by Inspr. Duncan, Linlithgow. Some slight damage was done in Kirkliston, one pane of glass in a window at 9 Queensferry Road, being broken by part of a nose cap and several telephone wires are down in the district. All this slight damage is believed to have been caused by the shrapnel from anti-aircraft fire.

'The final "Raiders Passed" signal was sounded about 4.35p.m. on the Port Edgar siren, followed by the local siren here. There were no air raid messages received by telephone at Port Edgar and they sounded all signals on hearing the Rosyth siren.'

You may remember that the Chief Constable in Edinburgh, Mr W. Morren had become aware of the raiders himself at 2.40p.m. His own report stated:

'At no time was any Air Raid Warning message received at this office. As instructed by the Scottish Home Department (Ministry of Home Security A.R.P. Department), I have lodged a complaint with the Chief Constable, Midlothian Constabulary, who is the Co-ordinating Officer for the Air Raid Warning System in this area, regarding the non-notification of an Air Raid Warning.'

Chief Constable Morren's report also listed twenty-three premises which had been struck by bullets and shell fragments. None of these properties were military and they were all definitely on dry land. Therefore, Hitler's personal order that no bombs should fall on British soil, as he didn't want to involve the civilian population, obviously didn't apply to machine-gun fire. The properties which were listed as struck, included a tailor's workshop, a laundry, Granton Gas Works, a football field, and seven private dwellings in Portobello; three of which were in Morton Street. Particularly riddled by shells was the Northern General Hospital, which reported damage in Wards Nos 1, 2 and 10, the recreation room and the nurses' quarters. As far as I can ascertain, nobody was injured in any of these rooms. Mind you, if they had been, they were certainly in a good place to be at the time. In fairness to the Germans, none of their bombs fell anywhere near dry land, so the shrapnel and shell fragments that seemed to be raining down on the city had almost certainly come from our own anti-aircraft defences. The ARP later reported that a bomb had been dropped in a field near Oakbank – on investigation this was discovered to be an AA shell. Also, many were of the opinion that the unusually large number of bullet holes in the area around the Portobello power station, were neither due to the Luftwaffe or the RAF – the Lewis gunners of the 94th City of Edinburgh Heavy Anti-Aircraft Regiment, looked decidely sheepish.

The most senior authority in terms of issuing air raid warnings, was Fighter Command Headquarters itself. Hugh Barkla, whom you may remember from earlier, was actually in the Filter Room at RAF Fighter Command Headquarters, Stanmore, at the time of the raid, and therefore quite a respectable authority on the subject, told us that Air Chief Marshal Dowding was well aware of the fact that a number of false alarms had caused problems during the day. In view of this, Dowding overrode the established procedure and held back. This is perhaps the singularly most important reason why no civilian sirens were sounded.

The Auxiliary Air Force were hugely unlucky. It's true enough that they made history by shooting down the first invaders over this country and in doing so won national acclaim, and legendary status. However, they were robbed of a much more significant victory. Robbed through outmoded tactics designed for biplane fighters, and a handicapping Fighter Command directive that ordered their guns to operate at a range of 400 yards. They were also robbed by incorrect tracking that sent their aircraft to the wrong places. The pilots themselves were ready, alert and keen to get into action. It was certainly not their fault that they were one step behind the enemy. They patrolled the areas to which they were sent, longing to be the first into action. It was like a huge cat and mouse game, that the Germans appeared to be winning. When contact was eventually made, the pilots of 602 and 603 Squadrons, entered combat with a gusto worthy of their now legendary status. Deservedly, their legend was born on that October afternoon, even though only two enemy aircraft were shot down.

The spirit of the Auxiliary Air Force, personified by Patsy Gifford, George Pinkerton, Archie McKellar, George Denholm, Douglas Farquhar, Jim Morton, 'Sheep' Gilroy, Finlay Boyd, Paul Webb, Ian Ferguson, Ken Macdonald, Colin Robertson, Sandy Johnstone, Dunlop Urie, Marcus Robinson, Hector MacLean, and all the other pilots who flew that day, still survives in the mind and heart of the modern Royal Auxiliary Air Force. It is therefore in my opinion, tremendously fitting that this book has been a combined effort between Group Captain Sir Hugh Dundas, an Auxiliary pilot from the time of this spiritual birth, and myself, Henry Buckton, a representative of the Royal Auxiliary Air Force of the 1990s.

Sir Hugh's connection to this work is all the more fitting when we consider his tremendous sublimity with the RAuxAF. Patsy Gifford, George Pinkerton and Archie McKellar, may well represent the Auxiliary spirit, but Group Captain Sir Hugh Dundas, *is* the Auxiliary Spirit. Arguably, the most famous and admired of those early auxiliary airmen, who through his family ties with the infant squadrons, exudes the character, style, charisma and make-up of that 'exclusive club'. In the introduction to this book I emphasised the influencing hand of destiny. It was certainly destiny that the foundations for this manuscript were re-discovered some thirty-five years after their creation. And certainly destiny that their creator was, in no uncertain terms, the persona of the Auxiliary Air Force itself.

The story of what happened on 16 October 1939 in my opinion makes excellent reading. If we were unaware of its historical accuracy, we may be inclined to suspect the way in which it happened, as a romantic fabrication of how the first air raid might have unfolded. In February 1957 Hugh Dundas was just about to start research on his book. At that point he didn't have the facts to hand, but he did have a romantic notion of how he would like to raid to appear in his narrative. He wrote a letter to Mr J. Nerney at the Air Historical Branch of the Air Ministry with an outline, which ultimately proved to be incredibly close to the truth.

> 'One idea has come to my mind and it is possible that you will be able to tell me whether it is feasible or not. As we know, the first enemy aircraft shot down over Britain were destroyed by the Auxiliaries of 602 and 603 Squadrons. Presumably we have a record of the names, ranks, etc., of the crew of those aircraft. I was thinking that it would be quite a dramatic start to the book if I began with a description of Hauptmann Blank? climbing into his Heinkel He 111. He is an experienced regular officer of the Luftwaffe. Possibly he has fought in Spain. He sets off on his mission against Scotland, full of confidence and training. Meanwhile, in a dispersal hut in Scotland there sit Flying Officers, X, Y and Z, farmer, solicitor and banker. At a certain point the two dissimilar elements meet, and bingo!
>
> 'This is just an idea which may not be borne out by facts anyway. But it does seem to me to be quite a dramatic way to emphasise in the very beginning of the book the advantages of possessing an Auxiliary Air Force.'

As we have already been witness, his dramatic illustration could not have been closer to the truth.

By the Spring of 1940, still before the official opening of the period which is commonly known as the Battle of Britain, Scotland continued to be one of the Luftwaffe's main targets. In a broadcast made on the BBC by the Secretary of State for Scotland the Rt. Hon. John Colville, PC, MP, said:

> 'Scotland has been much in the news of late – in the war news. German airmen seem to be very interested in what is going on there. They have paid rather dearly for their curiosity; in fact, well over half the total number of enemy planes which have been brought down in or around the coasts of Great Britain have met their fate off the Scottish coast or on Scottish soil.
>
> 'Any of you who are familiar with local government will know that in

Scotland we get eleven-eightieths of the English share of grants of money for certain services. Well, up to now we have certainly had more than our eleven-eightieths of the war so far as it has touched British shores. But we are not complaining. Fighting is not a new or unaccustomed thing for Scotland. From distant days we have been accustomed to fighting either with each other or with other people: the Celts and the Norsemen, the fights with the English, the old clan feuds, the Border raiders – names like Douglas, Elliot and Scott; the covenanters who held their conventicles on the bare Lowland hillsides while their armed pickets surrounded them to protect them from Claverhouse and his dragoons. Or, again, the soldiers of fortune who adventured into Scandinavia under the banner of Gustavus Adolphus, or who fought on the side of France under the Auld Alliance. These all go to make up the present race – Highland and Lowland – which today is united in strength and determination in the cause of freedom.

'Many men from the coasts and the islands are in the Navy or its auxiliary services, or in the Merchant Service, or are carrying on in their fishing boats despite the dirty methods of the Germans. The Outer Islands – the misty Hebrides – have sent a very high proportion of their men to sea, and some of these fine lads have given their lives in the nation's service. Some of them have been lost in fair and square battle at sea, and others have gone down before cowardly attacks. But Nazi airmen know by now how our fishermen and seamen react to their brutality. They now have the means to strike back, and they do so with courage and effect.

'It would do Dr Göbbels good to hear how a Clydeside engineer or fireman phrases his disgust and his determination to put an end to the dirty work. But such phrases are not for broadcasting. In addition to the little difficulty I might have with the BBC, I doubt if your receiving sets would stand the strain. I can, however, tell you about the grievance of a skipper whom I met recently who complained to me that he could not get into naval service on account of his age, and expressed his envy of other younger skippers who, as he put it, "We're awa' to a steady job at the mine-sweeping". Well, I ask my landsman friends to ponder over the courage of men like these – a steady job at the mine-sweeping, indeed!'

So, to whom does the story in this book belong? The answer to that question I suppose depends upon the readers and their particular prejudices. It belongs to the many individuals who took part in the action, either in the air or on the ground. It belongs to the people of Edinburgh, the people of Scotland, and the people of Great Britain. It belongs to the Royal Navy; in particular the officers and men of HMS *Mohawk* who died that day doing their job. These were all men who had joined the Royal Navy before the war had started. This fact is even more relevant today, with the closure of the Rosyth Naval Base in 1995. It belongs equally therefore to the German aircrew whose bodies went to a watery grave at the bottom of the Firth of Forth; and those who were buried at Portobello Cemetery with full military honours. It belongs to all those other services who, for good or bad reason, have cause to remember the Forth Raid as part of their internal history: the ambulance service, the police, the Air Raid Precaution Service, the AA gunners, the balloon barrage, etc.

Above all else, for me as the writer, the story belongs to the Spitfire. On Monday 25 March 1996 RAF Turnhouse closed down officially, and passed into the pages of history. A replica Spitfire which bears the markings of L.1070 (XT A), the aircraft which Flight Lieutenant Patrick (Patsy) Gifford of 603 (City of Edinburgh) Squadron, flew into immortality on 16 October 1939, stood guard outside the base, as a symbol of the bravery and sacrifice of the aircrew who fought and died in the name of freedom, and the preservation of liberty. During the closing ceremony for the station which had been operational for eighty glorious years, it was revealed by Sir John Harris, that the replica, by agreement of the RAF, MoD and Edinburgh District Council, would find a new home somewhere in the city and not be sent to another RAF base as feared.

For most of us today, Spitfires can only be seen in museums, like the RAF Museum at Hendon, or the Imperial War Museum at Duxford. Yet even here they seem to exude a magical aura. With a little imagination and undisturbed concentration, we can almost hear the rattle of the .303 Browning machine-guns; or hear Patsy Gifford calling 'Tally-ho' as he descends on Sigmund Storp's Ju 88 with all guns blazing; the confident smile of Archie McKellar as he exclaims 'I only came in for the dancing'; or the coolness of George Pinkerton as he continues to chase Helmut Pohle with empty guns. These men are all gone now, but a 'few' still remain. Group Captain Sir Hugh (Cocky) Dundas read the final manuscript to this book and wrote its foreword in May 1995. Two months later on 10 July 1995 he passed away. The men in this book, hold a special place in the history and heart of this country. Their struggle was unique, never before had such a small group of men held the destiny of millions in their grasp – and won. Never again will this type of battle be fought – no one will ever surpass their achievement, or their bravery.

Tribute in Memory of Group Captain Sir Hugh Dundas

CBE DSO DFC DL

22 July 1920 – 10 July 1995

The first time I saw Hugh Dundas was at Kirton in Lindsey in the winter of 1940-41: pink-cheeked, fair-haired, frequently smiling. He was tall, with what used to be called a cavalry stoop, a stance that imparted a certain nonchalance and implied a genial, easy-going approach to life. This contradicted the style he displayed with such distinction in the air, as both pilot and leader. He was popular then, remaining so throughout his career and was ultimately held in great admiration.

The apocryphal story about how he became known as 'Cocky' is not only absurd but, in its priapic implication, insulting and actionable. In his book *Flying Start*, he tells its true origin. It was another pilot in 616 Squadron, Teddy St Aubyn, who bestowed it. In the Mess ante-room one evening. Teddy, wanting a drink, pointed to him and said, 'Hey, you, Cocky, press the bell' (ring for a steward). When he asked why he had been thus addressed, the answer came, 'Because I couldn't remember your name and you look like a bloody great Rhode Island Red.'

Before the war, Auxiliary Air Force Officers used to wear a brass 'A' on each tunic lapel. In about the second year of the war this was replaced by a smaller 'A'; as a demonstration of independence, young Dundas wore one of each size which, someone said, made him look as though he were flying one wing low. Later the 'A' was abolished, but he ignored that edict too.

153

I did not come across him in North Africa, as I was in the Mediterranean Allied Coastal Air Force, but with Desert Air Force, in Italy I used to talk to him often on the R/T. He had an amusing precision when pin-pointing his position. At the head of a whole Wing flying at 15,000 ft: 'Crossing the Tagliamento River . . . . now!' He pronounced the name as though it were English, making no concessions to Italian.

A friend of mine on the Wing told me of a visit to a British officers' club, when Cocky turning up his cuffs to hide half his four rings, goaded a pompous Major with controversial comments, and, when his object was achieved and the infuriated pongo burst out with 'How dare you contradict your senior officer', with aplomb, Cocky turned down his cuffs to reveal his group captaincy.

He spoke admirably at the television shooting of Douglas Bader's *This Is Your Life*. My wife and I were at the studio, as our younger son is married to Douglas's elder step-daughter.

In the annals of air combat he is, of course, established as a fine pilot and great leader. He was also remarkably shrewd, outstandingly intelligent, and a most pleasant human being with an immense sense of humour.

Richard Bickers
April 1996

APPENDIX ONE

No. 603 City of Edinburgh (Fighter) Squadron
Nominal Roll of Officers as at 3 September 1939

RANK	NAME	CIVIL OCCUPATION
S/Leader	E.H. Stevens	Writer to the Signet
S/Leader	Rev. J. Rossie Brown	Chaplain
F/Lieut.	J.L. Jack	Bank Agent
F/Lieut.	I. Kirkpatrick	Writer to the Signet
F/Lieut.	P. Gifford	Solicitor
F/Lieut.	G.L. Denholm	Timber Merchant
F/Lieut.	I.A.G.L. Dick	Surgeon
F/Lieut.	T.C. Garden	Chartered Accountant
F/Officer	F.W. Rushmer	Electrical Engineer
F/Officer	H.K. Macdonald	Writer to the Signet
F/Officer	J.L.G. Cunningham	Grain Merchant
F/Officer	G.T. Wynne-Powell	Apprentice Chartered Accountant
F/Officer	J.G.E. Haig	Paper Maker
F/Officer	I.S. Ritchie	Writer to the Signet
F/Officer	J.A.B. Somerville	Bank Clerk
F/Officer	C.D. Peel	Apprentice Chartered Accountant
P/Officer	G.C. Hunter	Apprentice Chartered Accountant
P/Officer	G.K. Gilroy	Sheep Farmer
P/Officer	J.S. Morton	Mining Engineer
P/Officer	D.K.A. Mackenzie	Apprentice Chartered Accountant
P/Officer	W.A. Douglas	Student
A/P/O	C.E. Hamilton	Student
Pupil Pilot	R. Mackay	Travel Agent

Appendix Two

Operations Record Book
Detail of work carried out by No. 603 Squadron
From 1430 hrs 16/10/39 to 1630 hrs 16/10/39

Aircraft Type and No.	Crew	Time Up	Time Down
Spitfires			
L.1070	F/LT. P. Gifford	1430	1455
L.1050	P/O. C. Robertson	1430	1500
L.1061	F/O. H.K. Macdonald	1430	1500
L.1067	F/LT. G.L. Denholm	1435	1455
L.1049	P/O. J.S. Morton	1435	1455
L.1048	P/O. G.K. Gilroy	1435	1455
L.1050	P/O. C. Robertson	1540	1630
L.1049	P/O. J.S. Morton	1600	1615
L.1021	F/O. J.L.G. Cunningham	1445	1600
L.1020	P/O. B.J.G. Carbury	1445	1600
L.1022	P/O. C.D. Peel	1430	1520
L.1024	F/O. F.W. Rushmer	1445	1600
L.1026	F/O. G.T. Wynne-Powell	1455	1555
L.1046	F/O. J.C. Boulter	1455	1600

INDEX

157